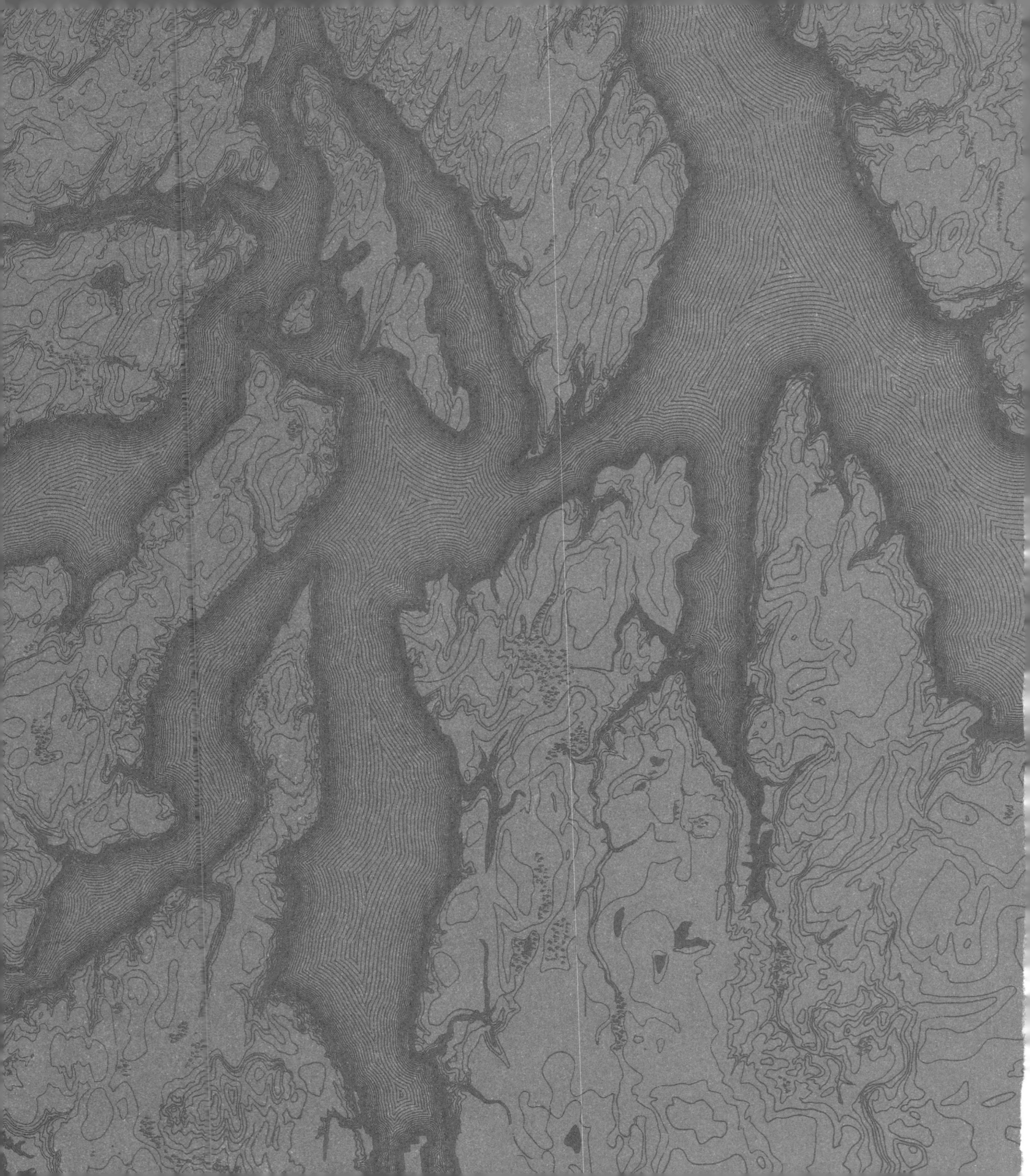

WESTLAND DISTILLERY

OUR WEST IS WHISKEY

TEN YEARS OF EXPLORING PROVENANCE
IN AMERICAN SINGLE MALT WHISKEY

2011 — 2021

FIRST EDITION

Copyright © 2021 by The Westland Distillery Company Ltd.

This book was produced and published by:
The Westland Distillery Company Ltd.
2931 1st Avenue South, Suite B
Seattle, Washington 98134
www.westlanddistillery.com

All rights reserved. No part of this publication may be reproduced or transmitted in any form or by any means, electronic or mechanical, including photocopy, recording or any information storage or retrieval system, without permission in writing from the publisher.

ISBN: 978-0-578-91344-5

Written by Matt Hofmann, Steve Hawley, and Nate Manny unless otherwise noted.
Edited by Steve Hawley
Design and illustration by Nate Manny and Jason Thornton at 51 Eggs
Book design by Nate Manny at 51 Eggs

Photography by:
Carson Artac: *11, 20 (BR), 25, 27, 36, 48, 50, 61, 63, 65, 68, 69, 72, 73, 77, 79, 82, 83, 86, 89, 94-95, 97, 104, 129, 132-133, 134 (TL, TR, BM, BR), 145 (BR), 149, 151, 154, 155, 157-158, 160, 161, 163, 167-168, 171 (T), 172, 181, 186, 200, 201, 206 (T), 207-211, 223, 227-228, 231 (T, BR), 232, 235, 237*
Bobby Biskupiak: *144 (T)*
Getty Images: *121, 125, 128*
Travis Gillett: *206 (B)*
Steve Hawley: *1, 3, 7, 9, 15, 19 (BL), 20 (T, BL), 21, 22, 23, 51, 55, 56 (T), 57, 58, 59, 119, 134 (TM), 143, 170*
Kyle Johnson: *45, 169, 193, 321 (BL)*
Tyler Kalberg: *145 (TR), 146 (R)*
Pat Kehoe: *144 (B), 173*
Frank Lamb Archive: *19 (TL, R), 44*
Nate Manny: *31, 37, 39, 41, 42, 107, 110 (B), 135, 147 (B)*
Stuart Mullenberg: *175*
Don Milgate: *109, 110 (TL), 112-114, 138-140, 141, 145 (TL), 146 (L), 147 (T), 148, 171 (B), 205*
Plains of Yonder: *234*
Polson Museum Archive: *213, 216, 217, 220, 221-222*
Carina Skrobecki: *134 (BL)*
Nick Strohmeyer: *233*
Robert Weyrick: *56 (B)*

Printed in China

TABLE OF CONTENTS

PART ONE:
SETTING OUT
- 4   Dead Reckoning
- 10   Whiskey Or Whisky?
- 12   Our West Is Whiskey
- 16   Leaving A Record

PART TWO:
THE PROMISE OF THE WEST
- 32   Our New West
- 38   The Treecoil
- 43   Something To Live Up To
- 46   American Oak
- 52   A Proving Ground

PART THREE:
RECONNECTING WHISKEY TO AGRICULTURE
- 66   Stewarding Our Living Heritage
- 74   Breeding A Revolution
- 84   Planting A New Seed
- 90   The Hunt for Garry Oak
- 98   Possibility In Variety
- 108   The Week Of Reek

PART FOUR:
CULTURAL TERROIR
- 122   Inspiration And Influences
- 131   Kindred Spirits
- 136   Brothers In Barley
- 142   All Kidding Aside
- 150   New Roads Through Andalucía
- 162   Sustainability In Whiskey

PART FIVE:
WHISKEY FOR A NEW WORLD
- 176   Unveiling Whiskey
- 182   Seeking Possibilities In Single Malt
- 188   The Birth Of A Category
- 194   The Pace Of Progress

PART SIX:
EPILOGUE
- 214   A Sermon From The Deacon Seat
- 224   Into The Unknown

PART ONE

SETTING OUT

"What lies behind us and what lies before us are tiny matters compared to what lies within us."

—

Ralph Waldo Emerson

DEAD RECKONING

by Matt Hofmann

What you will find in this book is a collection of essays with a loose narrative structure that spans the past ten years. Though you should not view the whole as completely linear, it does make sense to begin this journey with a look at the beginning, at the founding of Westland. It is by far the most difficult essay to write and I've saved it for last.

This might sound absurd, but I don't really know when Westland was founded. When was the moment of conception? What does it mean to found something, really? I downloaded my first whiskey production textbook at 15 years old when my childhood obsession with flavor met the alchemy of distillation. It was then that the idea of becoming a distiller first came into my mind. I bought my first still in 2007 at 18 years old and my second at 19, when the idea had snowballed into something of an obsession. After a year of college, linking up with a high school friend, Emerson Lamb, turbocharged the obsession into a real question that we posed to the TTB: What prevents two 19-year-olds from starting a distillery?

They laughed. But we were serious. To their credit, they responded thoughtfully and actually provided the rationale. Impatient as we were, we knew we needed to wait until we were 21 years old. So, we kept learning, absorbing information as fast as we could, and constantly building. In hindsight, the sheer amount of work we put in, the series of steps we took, is still eye-opening to me.

In September of 2008 we attended our first proper distillation course at Michigan State University. We drove there from Seattle, a multi-day journey. The trip was punctuated by news on the radio of Lehman Brothers going bankrupt and the Dow collapsing by the hour. Still enrolled at the University of Washington, I returned from Michigan three weeks after classes began for the fall quarter. I was assigned to a group in my accounting course with a woman who was wondering (rightfully), "Who the hell shows up to school three weeks late?" That woman is now my wife.

Weekends at Mason Lake followed. There, at a property Emerson's family owned, we stripped out an old boat house (read: garage) and built up a new distillery, fully equipped to distill single malt whiskey over the course of the following summer in 2009. Emerson's mechanical skillset, talent, and work ethic turned a collection of distilling equipment into a distillery. Meanwhile, I was still experimenting with refining technique and ingredients that would one day turn into core components of our house style: roasted malts, brewer's yeast, and new American oak. In the fall of 2009, I dropped out of the University of Washington to move out to Mason Lake and focus my attention on making whiskey full time.

Distilling experimental batches through the winter, 2009 quickly turned into spring of 2010. With Emerson's father, David, now on board with the idea that this was going to turn into a real company, we headed off to Europe. The two primary stops we made on that trip added further momentum to our early journey—experiencing single malt on Islay, Scotland and buying our first still from Christian Carl in Germany. While we were doing this, I was adding some formal distilling education to my "self-taught" knowledge bank by enrolling in classes with the Institute of Brewing and Distilling in London, as well as Heriot-Watt University in Edinburgh.

We secured our business license in September of 2010 and soon acquired the assets of an extremely small distilling company called Smith and Sullivan. The opportunity to begin commercial production in a facility that was already fully licensed gave us an invaluable head start. By the end of the year, we began working with Steve Hawley and Nate Manny to help us translate our original vision and ethos into a living, breathing brand. In May of 2011, our still arrived from Germany and we distilled our first batch of whiskey on June 21st, 2011.

So, what does it mean to "found" a company? Does it mean to be there at the beginning? When is the beginning, exactly? At the core of Westland has always been the idea that there is more to be explored in single malt whiskey. The simplest concept of Westland's founding moment is when we moved from distilling experimentation into concrete actions to develop a business, which Emerson and I did beginning in 2008. But is the point of origin nearly two years later when we secured our business license in September of 2010? Or is June of 2011 when spirit first began to flow from our Christian Carl still? For us, it is this last milestone that is the seminal one, so we are choosing to use this date to mark ten official years as a distillery in 2021.

> *"What makes a moment 'foundational'? To me, it's when the stakes are high and a new vision is established..."*

To be fair, founding Westland has always been more complex than just two people at a given date in time saying, "Westland is hereby founded!" There were so many people who helped us in those early days, in particular David Lamb, who provided the funding for this crazy adventure. There have been many more who have helped indirectly as well, including some of the authors in this book. Ultimately, I like to think there are foundational moments that have happened along the way, and are still happening today.

What makes a moment "foundational"? To me, it's when the stakes are high and a new vision is established, or the pathway is altered with a strong, emotional belief that there is possibility ahead. This happens at the founding of a company, yes, but also at a variety of inflection points along the way whose importance become more and more apparent over time. To found a company, any company, or to make a foundational change in one, is to make a leap of faith, a bet on both an idea and yourself that something new is possible.

The beauty of Westland, in my eyes, is that we've maintained an entrepreneurial tension. It's in our DNA. Our modus operandi is described elsewhere in this book as "perpetual forward motion." Growth happens along the uncertain path. The idea of exploring our west, whiskey, means we're constantly on the edge of the unknowable. As a result, we must cling to a belief in something that is possible but not yet manifested, all the while knowing it's up to us to make that happen.

It's exhausting. There are days when I'm just tired, the emotional roller coaster too much to handle day in, day out. But it's also thrilling in a way that I can't describe. It would be so much easier to move to Scotland and make "traditional" single malt whiskey or settle in Kentucky to produce Bourbon. I just can't ever see myself doing that. I'm addicted to the tension. It makes me feel alive and at home.

It helps to have a team that can carry the load, especially in the most extreme moments. Emerson left the business in 2015, but both before and after his departure we've naturally attracted, then eventually targeted, employees and partners who would feel engaged in those foundational moments. In particular, Steve and Nate have been huge contributors to Westland over the past ten years, and they're the central driving forces behind this book as well. They have both gone from acquaintances helping us describe the work we're doing to becoming active participants with emotional investment and leaders in this endeavor. Both add pieces to the business that expand the idea itself. Many others have since followed in the same way.

This book is about the past ten years and also a glimpse into where we're headed next. We've likened it to a time capsule. To those of you reading the contents found within, I hope you enjoy the recollections, the insights, and the perspective on what has been an incredible first decade. To those of you that have been a part of the foundational moments we've been through thus far, I can't thank you enough. To those of you who will be a part of those foundational moments to come for this company, even many years after we're long gone, fate willing, I would say: Do not be afraid to step out into the unknown to find our new West. This is what it means to be Westland.

WHISKEY OR WHISKY?

by Steve Hawley

From Day One we had a fundamental choice to make: Would we be a whisky distillery or a whiskey distillery? The former would signal unequivocally that we are makers of single malt and tie us to a centuries-old tradition. The latter would signal that we are distinctly American and root us in new world ideals. Unsurprisingly, we chose to identify with the American vernacular.

Neither variation is wrong and throughout this book you'll see both spellings. This is intentional. Rather than impose our choice on others, we've honored the preference of the author, along with other regional idiosyncrasies of English language, even when they diverge from our rules.

What you will absolutely not see in this book is the dreadful "whisk(e)y." This is an affront to good taste and a clumsy new custom we vehemently oppose in all circumstances. After all, elegance is not only something to strive for in the whiskey itself, but also in the language that accompanies it.

OUR WEST IS WHISKEY

by Matt Hofmann

The West. Two words with dramatically different cultural interpretations depending on where in the world the thought is conjured. To many, it is no more than a cardinal direction. To some, a historical nemesis, or even an enemy. To still more, a way of describing a civilization with a prescribed structure. To us, home.

Each different image of the West can be valid. But when it comes time for us, here in this place that we call the American West, to represent that idea of home, there is an additional level of responsibility. For we are the custodians of all we inherit, and this culture is truly ours to examine meticulously, participate in vigorously, preserve with integrity, and improve thoughtfully when called upon.

Describing the West to someone of another culture can prove challenging. For too long it has often been depicted as a caricature of itself, replete with cowboy hats, iced-over beards, or yes, flannel. It can be more challenging still to describe it to someone living within it, contributing to the tapestry with their own single strand of fiber that represents their lived truth, yet perhaps unable, uninterested, or unconvinced that creating the larger pattern is of consequence. Such is the challenge of interpreting a living culture. But any living culture has sprouted from something, ours being no exception.

People moved to this place seeking something. Their motivations ranged from the fundamental and primal to the ambitious and creative. "The West" has become the domain of iconoclasts seeking an alternative to conventional ways. Here we have explored new ways to source food, built communities rooted in unique values, escaped oppression, conquered wilderness. With its bountiful resources, the West has served as a blank canvas on which to redefine oneself and your way of interacting with the world. All valid interpretations, yet different manifestations, growing from the same seed.

To us, the West represents opportunity, possibility, curiosity, confidence, and idealism. Out of this fertile ground of history, lived experiences, and shared culture has emerged our clear vision:

Our West is Whiskey.

We see this place, this beautiful, stunning place, as ideal for a new style of single malt whiskey. River valleys and plains shaped by fire and water, by the crude rock born of volcanic eruptions in eons past, tempered by millennia of ice sheets and rainfall, have become renowned as some of the most fertile soils on Earth. This, paired with a climate anchored in slow but steady precipitation, punctuated by the piercing blue skies of summer, provides the perfect conditions for growing barley. If you believe that whiskey should reflect the agriculture of the place where it is made, as we do, the West is ripe with possibilities. Yet what we see in our West is still more opportunity.

In whiskey itself, as a discipline, we do not see a fully explored, mature world, as most in our industry do. We see the opposite. An occupation hundreds of years old passively formed by the mundane, cumulative impact of legal statutes, technological advancements, fuel availability, trade balances, and even taxation. Weathered stone, sculpted by time, protected from future erosion or improvement by a narrative buffer that benefits from the rock staying exactly as it is. While our Western culture zealously values the preservation of the nature around us, with equal fervor do we insist on improving ourselves and our way of being within it. For us, whiskey is not a feature of this world that is ours to protect, it is an extension of ourselves that is ours to advance when the opportunity presents itself.

"Whiskey is not a feature of this world that is ours to protect, it is an extension of ourselves that is ours to advance..."

And the opportunities are vast, maybe incalculable. To understand our approach to a subject of this scale, it may be best to focus on how we handle the heart of single malt whiskey: malted barley. We've looked at malt from different perspectives over the past ten years, asking new questions about the things we notice at each new vantage point.

Upon first contact, we began with: "What kinds of flavors are possible from malted barley that aren't being explored today?" A glance at this ingredient from the perspective of the brewing industry was all it took to find some exciting answers to that question, which wasn't even being asked in our own industry.

A few years later came a new perspective, this time informed by the wine industry, that led to a new question: "What about differences in variety of barley?" Partly driven by this answer, the next perspective derived from an examination of how we grow barley and of the impact of farming and sustainable agricultural practices. As of this writing, the newest perspective demands an almost outrageous question: "Is our industry's current definition of malted barley even correct?" Ten years have past and we have circled the topic of malted barley again and again, each time sensing an opportunity to approach it from a new perspective. But always, we're heading west.

To us, the West is both the physical place we call home but also a mindset, an ethos. It is the edge of the world, literally but not figuratively. While the land ends, our imagination and ambition does not. We approach the discipline of whiskey-making with this philosophy at heart, as if we could really do it any other way. The impact that this has on us as a whiskey distillery is immense. Whereas many in our industry idolize the stationary past, our exploration of possibility results in perpetual motion. There is not an end goal we are trying to reach. I doubt there even is an end. The journey is the objective for us, and the whiskeys we release are snapshots of what we're uncovering along the way.

For as much as we've studied malted barley over the last decade, we've done the same for most other parts of single malt whiskey production, the examples too numerous to describe here. Curiosity compels us to explore further, sometimes to seek answers and other times to find new questions to ask. Out here, on the edges of whiskey's unknown, we do not find safety and comfort, nor do we seek it. Out here, we see opportunity and find possibility, the key to our restless hearts. Out here, in the West, we feel at home.

15 | OUR WEST IS WHISKEY

LEAVING A RECORD

by Steve Hawley

Beginning in 2011, our small but industrious team began issuing Quarterly Reports to a small but influential community of friends, mentors, pundits, partners, and future customers. Packaged simply in a small wooden box, these reports consisted of a sample of our whiskey in the making (what would eventually become Deacon Seat) and a formal review of the happenings at a distillery still being shaped, both spiritually and physically.

On the face of it, the idea was simple: let those that have helped us along the way share in the experience we had the privilege to live every day. But while each bottle served as a window into Westland's emerging house style, the whiskeys belied a greater intent. These reports were really meant to forge lasting connections and build an ardent community, to instill in us as much as them a fervent anticipation for a rewarding future to come.

In truth, these Quarterly Reports were the first tangible things we put out into the world that bore the Westland name and brand. It set a bar, of sorts, for the thoughtfulness we would bring to each and every action moving forward. In an industry where many were throwing themselves recklessly into whiskey, at a time when many were cutting corners, we carried on with eyes set on higher ground. We heard what became a familiar refrain from those who received the reports, "You guys are doing it right." And that was enough to steel our resolve.

In the time since the last Quarterly Report was created in the winter of 2014, these modest wooden boxes have become treasured artifacts—the first entries in the record of the Westland story. While many more artifacts have since been added, expanding the account, a full collection of these initial reports offers the most complete picture of the dawning of an idea.

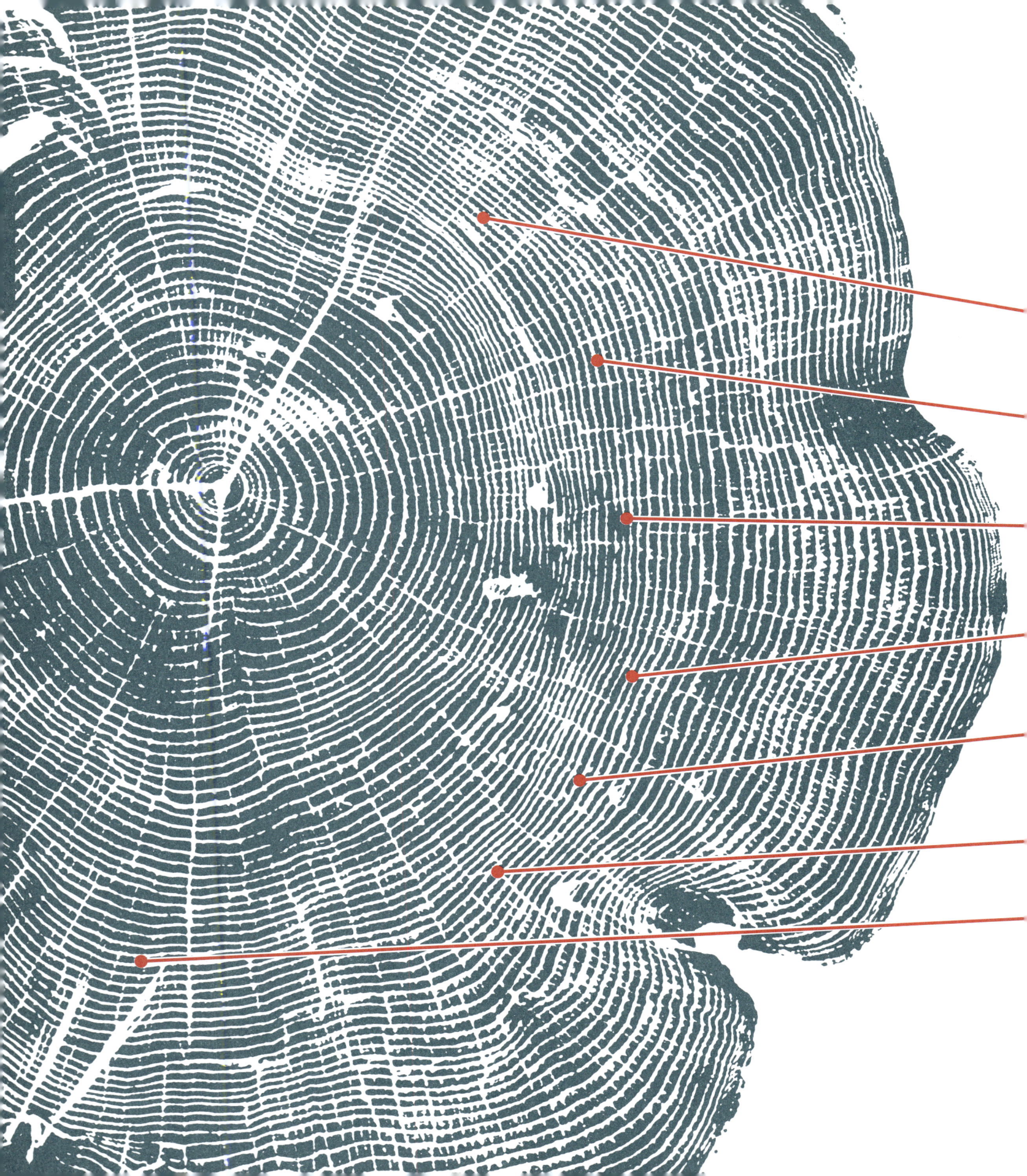

FIRST DAYS

The early years were filled with a tempest of emotions, from thrilled anticipation, to thoughtful contemplation, to nearly crippling anxiety. We had our vision to cling to and a steadfast belief in ourselves. As we set out into what was largely unknown to us, and in some aspects unknowable to anyone, we simply reminded ourselves that if we kept our heads down and focused on what we thought to be compelling, the world would soon open up for us.

1. MARCH 2010: PILGRIMAGE TO SCOTLAND

Matt and Emerson traveled to the birthplace of single malt (many would argue) to soak themselves in its provenance and history and come to understand on a visceral level how whiskey can be evocative of a place.

2. SEPTEMBER 2010: COMPANY FOUNDING

If the completion of a first formal business plan constitutes a company's origin, then this date deserves to be enshrined.

3. FEBRUARY 2011: DSP LICENSING

If, on the other hand, one requires the official sanction by a government body to consider a business fully established, we recognize this date.

4. MARCH 2011: FIRST PROTOTYPE

None that know us will be surprised to learn that our first prototype single malt was remarkably quick to follow our licensing. Mason Lake Malt was becoming Westland American Single Malt.

5. MAY 2011: FIRST STILL ARRIVAL

Our Christian Carl still arrived on the shores of the mighty Duwamish River. Our team would spend the next month hard at work, day and night, commissioning our new system with little thought and less regard for anything else happening in the world, save perhaps for the impending arrival of the next generation.

6. JUNE 2011: FIRST COMMERCIAL DISTILLATION

We celebrate ten years now from the date spirits first flowed from a commercial still at Westland. Our journey was officially underway, and the long wait began.

7. NOVEMBER 2011: FIRST CASK OF GARRY OAK FILLED

It wasn't long before we began choosing paths that took us further and further away from old world conventions. As it was our first foray, Garryana will always hold a special place in our souls.

THE PROGRESS OF WESTLAND 2010–2011

19 | OUR WEST IS WHISKEY

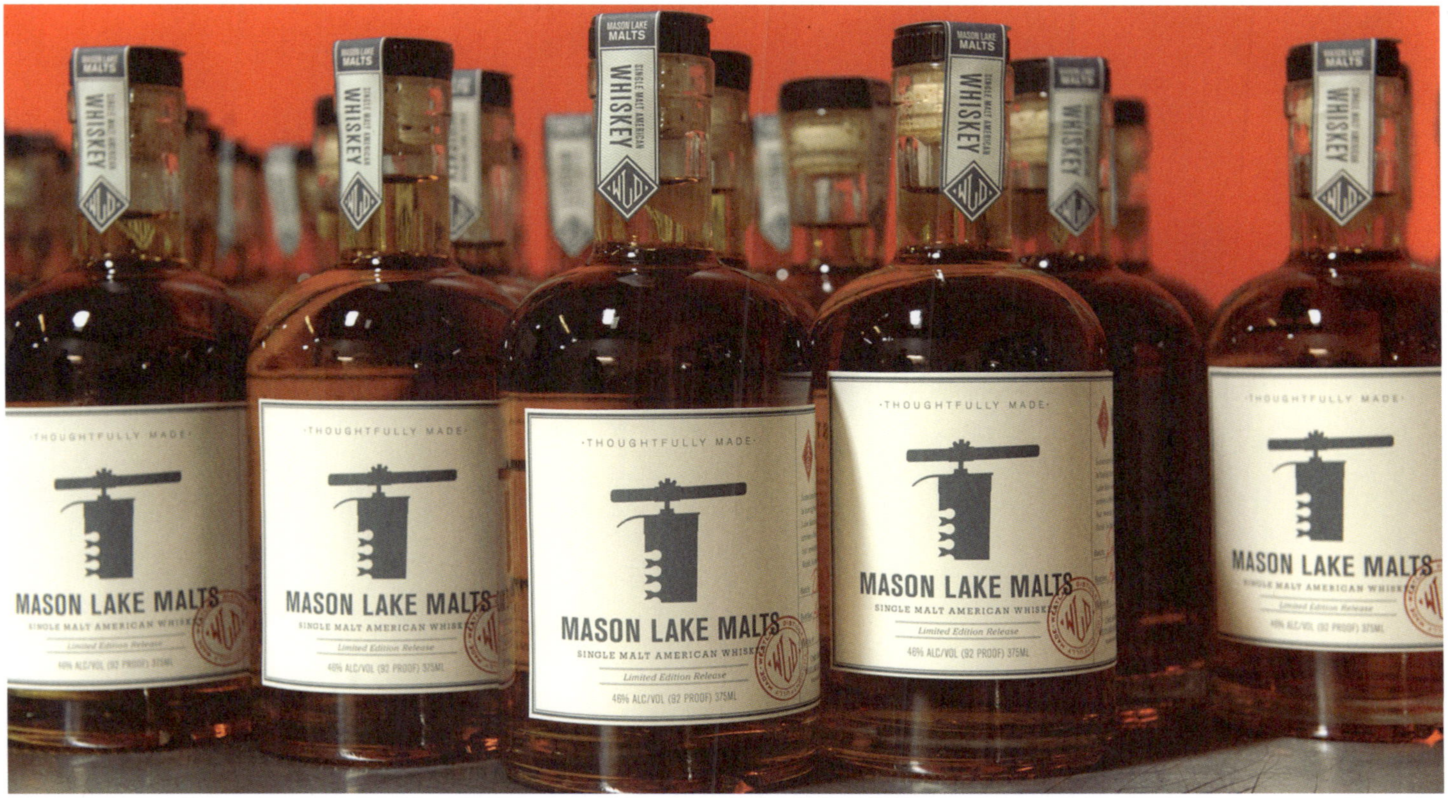
MASON LAKE MALTS
SINGLE MALT AMERICAN WHISKEY
THOUGHTFULLY MADE
MASON LAKE MALTS
SINGLE MALT AMERICAN WHISKEY
Limited Edition Release
46% ALC/VOL (92 PROOF) 375ML

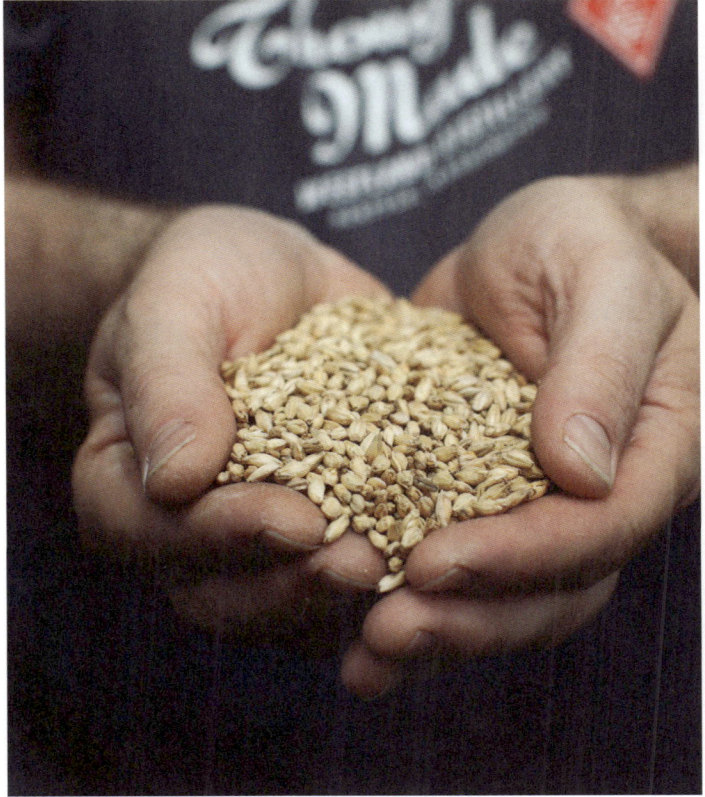

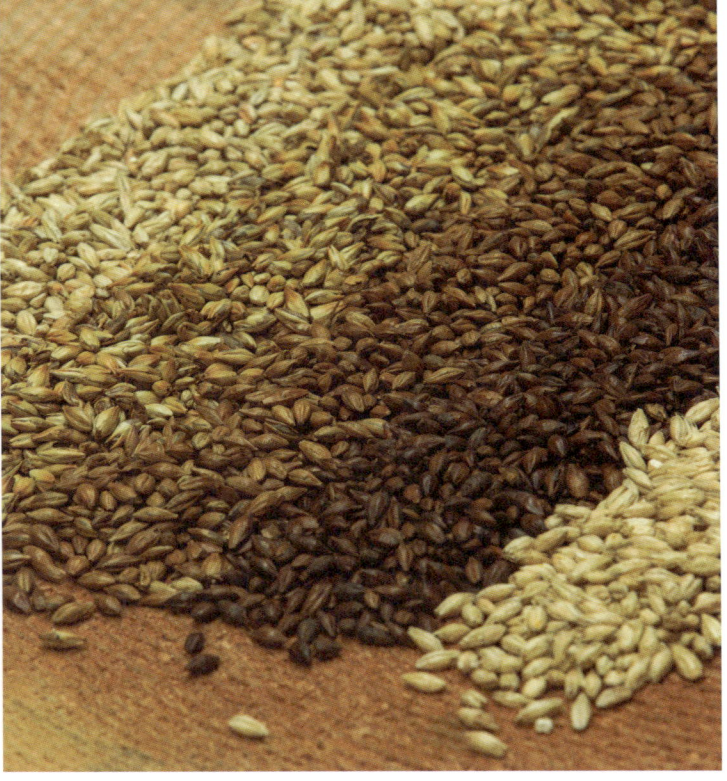

21 | OUR WEST IS WHISKEY

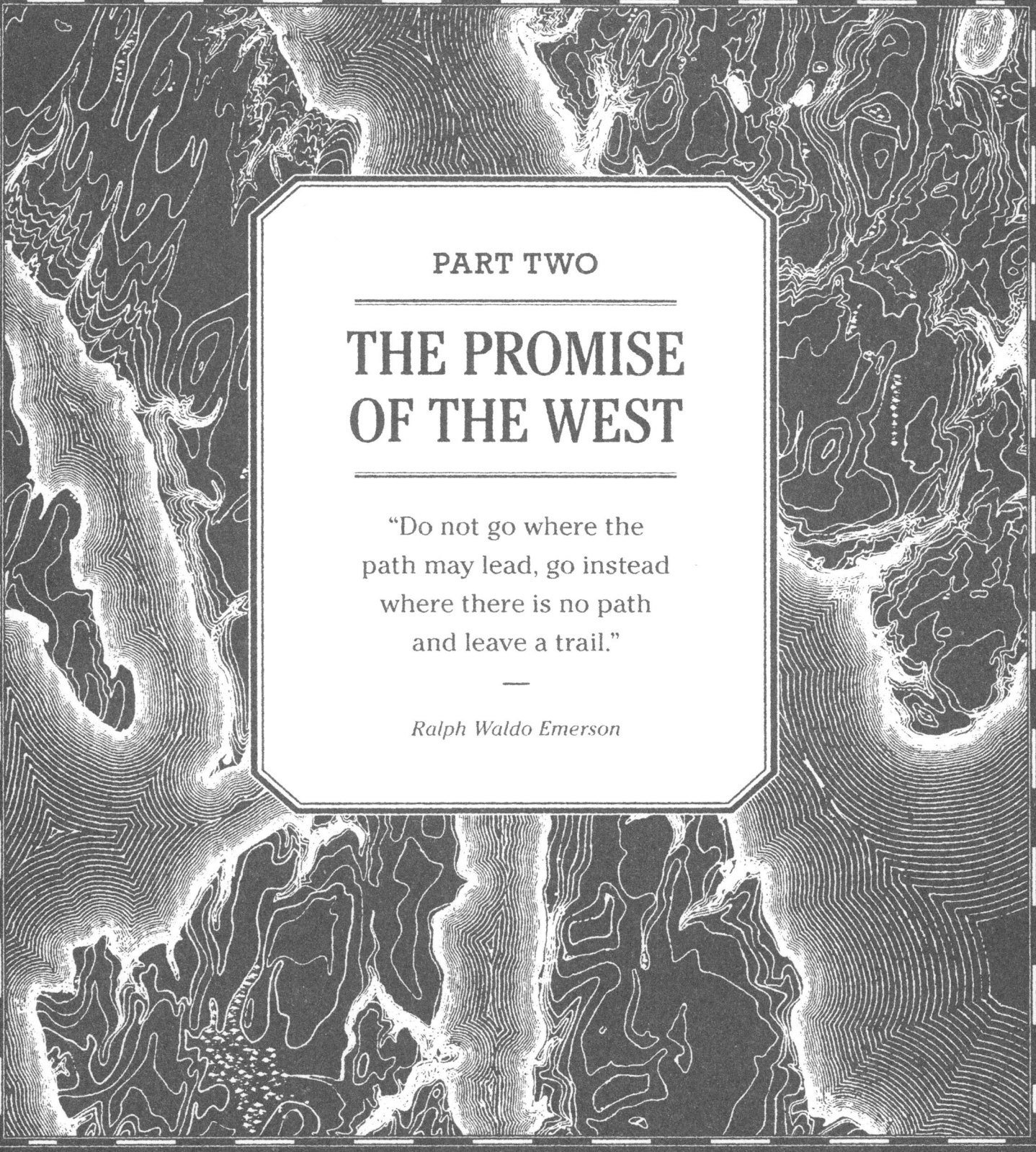

PART TWO

THE PROMISE OF THE WEST

"Do not go where the path may lead, go instead where there is no path and leave a trail."

—

Ralph Waldo Emerson

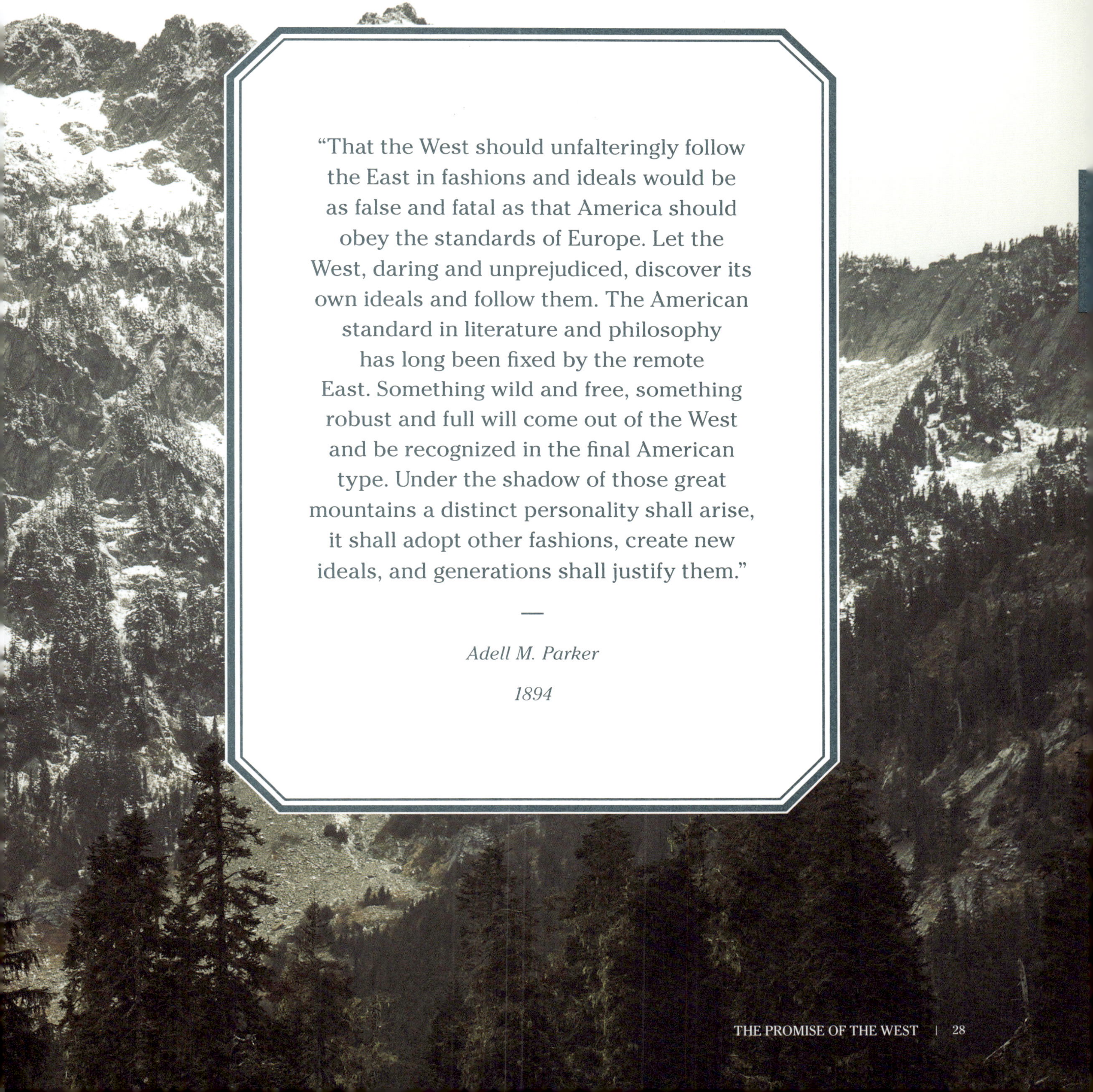

"That the West should unfalteringly follow the East in fashions and ideals would be as false and fatal as that America should obey the standards of Europe. Let the West, daring and unprejudiced, discover its own ideals and follow them. The American standard in literature and philosophy has long been fixed by the remote East. Something wild and free, something robust and full will come out of the West and be recognized in the final American type. Under the shadow of those great mountains a distinct personality shall arise, it shall adopt other fashions, create new ideals, and generations shall justify them."

—

Adell M. Parker

1894

WESTLAND

Westland sits at the edge of the new world. While there is no further land to tread, most certainly there still remains new territory to explore. Freed from the confines of convention and far removed from the expectations of the old world, we set forth from this place unencumbered, save for a mandate to live up to the promise of the West.

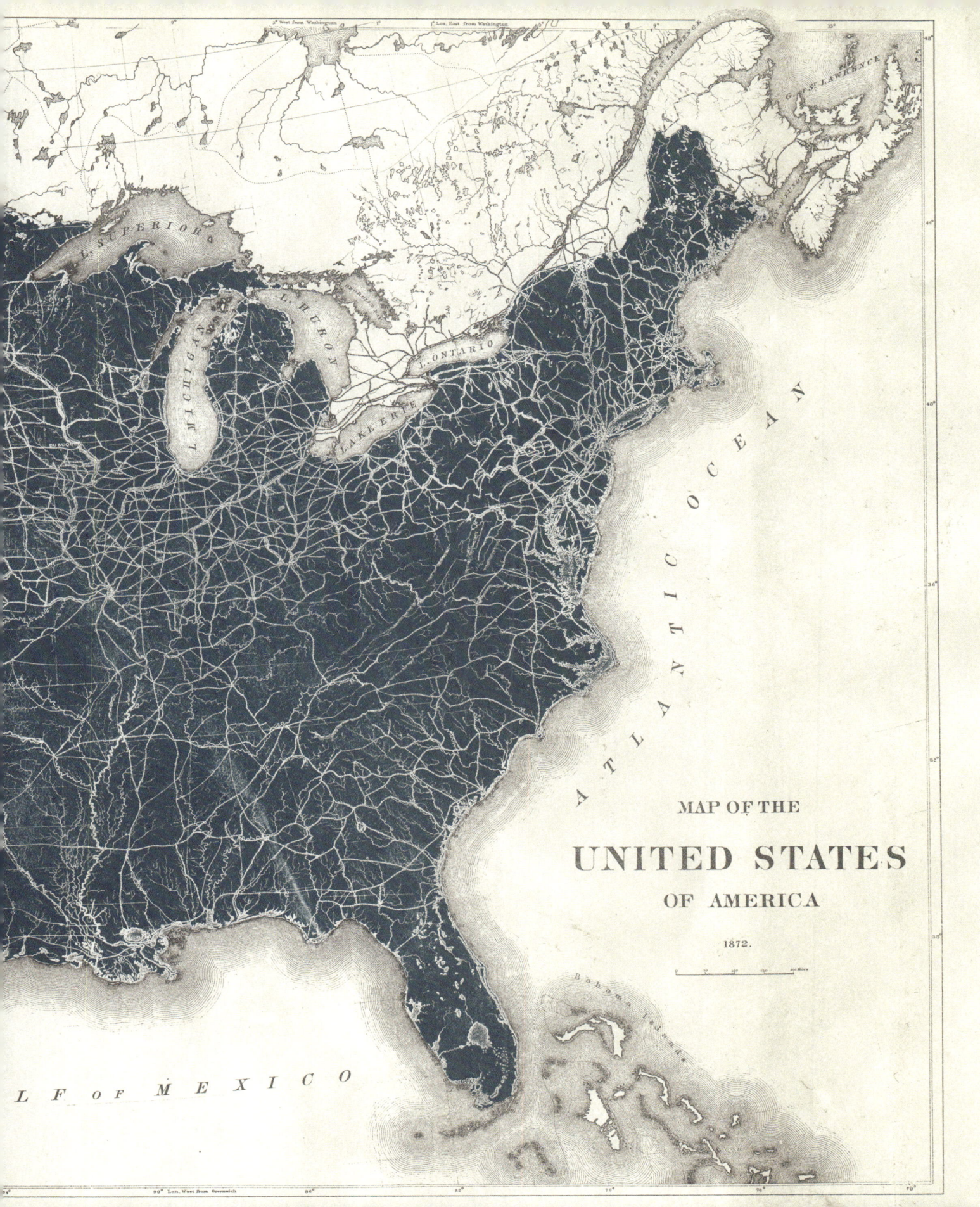

OUR NEW WEST

by Nate Manny

Few ideas have maintained their grip so fiercely upon the imagination, or had such broad interpretation as that of "The West." Its definition, amorphous and sprawling, continues to be sculpted in real time, moving perpetually from boom to boom and horizon to horizon. As dynamic as it is restless, its only constants have been that it never stops reinventing itself, that perseverance and hard work are essential to survival and success in it, and that its influence is continually giving new shape to our world.

Made famous as the land of huge open spaces, impenetrable forests, treacherous mountains, and swift rivers full of gold nuggets waiting to be plucked from their beds, this was the hard Wild West of yesteryear. Beyond the edge of the known world, it was a vast territory, raw and waiting to be explored. This picturesque landscape and the tales of the people who travailed, lived, and died within it have created some of the most enduring legends of our times.

But it is the promise of the West, more than the reality of it, that has driven a sea change of thought and action for nearly 700 years. Throughout its long and complicated history, it is this aspect that has been the most infectious—that the West is a land of new ideas and possibility. A place for outside voices to be heard and for new ones to be realized. A place to build new infrastructures and develop new ways of being. It has offered the rare chance to start anew, to define oneself on their own terms, and to live free while giving form to the new world. The West has long stood as a beacon of hope and opportunity for those who have had the wherewithal and resolve to endeavor here.

For generations, the West has provided an aspirational destination both on a map and in the minds of people everywhere. But as the frontiers of the unknown have conjoined with the edges of the familiar, we now find ourselves in a new era—one in which the idea of the West has once again transformed to take on a new significance.

Today the West is not a physical place but an ethos. Here, the West's first constant—that of perpetual motion and reinvention—still defies the complicity of discovered and established civilization but in a different way than it has in the past. While today the immensity is easier for us to traverse physically, the New West connects us to the past through a shared understanding that there is always opportunity waiting if we have the courage and audacity to pursue it. It gives us hope and validates our sense of purpose. It motivates us to explore and to pursue our ambition. This hope and sense of purpose are the innate forces that push us to

The logo is an amalgamation of several ideas forged into a single mark and rendered in a way, like in our era of reference, that it can be made with the impact of a single tool. The tree represents the history of the logging industry in the Lamb family, but also the growth of a new endeavor for the future; the roots of that tree take the form of the condensing coils of a still. The style in which these elements are rendered is inspired by the branding hammers used by lumber companies to mark the ends of felled trees and to indicate ownership before they went downriver to the saw mill; another nod to the history of our origins, but also to our era of reference.

As a mark, The Treecoil has proven to be both versatile and durable—it has been carved, cast, printed, sewn, stenciled, branded, embossed, and embroidered—but it always maintains its integrity and does its job of identifying Westland.

SOMETHING TO LIVE UP TO

by Steve Hawley

It's not enough to simply have a calling. You must navigate the journey to your ambitions—one that, for us in whiskey, has no final destination. To set our course, we often begin by simply putting pen to paper. As evidenced by this book, we hold dear the practice of writing at Westland and we commit ourselves faithfully to the discipline.

The manifesto sits at the heart of our routine. Opposite this page is not our first manifesto, but one of our earliest writings and the origins of our mantra, *Thoughtfully Made*. It served as a guide that marked our ambitions at a moment in time; a compass that pointed us in the right direction from the place where we stood.

When we're in the work there's a second-hand language that emerges. Quickened over time, we each have come to understand the nature of the work and the nature of each other. But it's important not to take that for granted. As we reach each new outpost, so we must memorialize the moment and reset the collective ambition. We must identify a new point on the horizon through words we can together embrace before recalibrating our compass. These aren't mere marketing slogans or platitudes. Manifestos stir us to the wonders of our endeavor and give us something to live up to.

WE ARE THE CUSTODIANS OF ALL WE INHERIT

Before a mountain range was crossed, before a railroad was built, before the dark wall of a forest was breached, a rare few stood before these obstacles and declared, "I can." Our own pursuit is inspired by the doers of things, our ethic in step with theirs. While the courage to believe in possibility is the necessary first step, it is the willingness and wherewithal to act that harnesses the power of a river and turns it into light, or distills a mash into a fine whiskey.

A thing of true quality derives from an ethic rooted in process. For us, it's knowing that whiskey is more than spirit in a bottle; it's the essence of everything that went into its creation. Our whiskey is built on the collective knowledge of the generations that preceded us. From the craftsman who forged the stills, to the farmers who have grown our malted barley, to the life's work of master distillers that came before us. It is through their example that we learn how a thing is done right.

It is now our responsibility to lay our stone in the wall of history. To pursue our own truths, to define a new vision of greatness that is unique to our time and place, expressed in a whiskey, "Thoughtfully Made."

AMERICAN OAK

by Steve Hawley

Nearly everyone sees the romance in whiskey. I won't pretend it's not an honest portrayal of the life. But many also lament the patience it calls for, the long years between inspiration and the bottle. It's been asked of us more than once, "Making whiskey sounds incredible, but how can you stand to wait so long to find out if an idea will work out?" The truth is, an idea doesn't only have a genesis and a conclusion. It is in every way a pursuit—something you're able to inhabit, to witness unfold, and to shape over the long stretches of time so few have the patience for. While the bottom line often beckons, there is no singular end point you're beholden to.

Certainly, this maxim is not the sole domain of whiskey makers. If you're willing to be open and present, it is true of any vocation. But whiskey is unique in that the life of an idea is manifest over time in tangible, sensorial ways. And rarely does it take the path of linear steps to a predetermined vision of the end. I spent much of my life before Westland working in the trade of ideas. The goal was to devise creative solutions to identified problems. In almost every case, the ideas we conceived remained just that—conceptions. They were theories, frameworks, plans, methodologies, messages, scripts, and transient artwork destined for a passing glance on a screen. Whiskey is different. The arc of an idea plays out over years in stages you can actually smell, touch, and taste. It literally seeps into your clothes. There is a level of ongoing empirical feedback that doesn't exist in the purely human economies that dominate our world today. Changes are observable. Insights palpable. Whiskey speaks back in a way people can't. An idea in whiskey physically unfolds in front of you.

For me, American Oak, our flagship whiskey to this point in time, is a living manifestation of an idea more so than it is simply a whiskey in a bottle. It is not a solution to a problem, it's an answer to a question.

Undoubtedly, American Oak stands as our greatest departure from Scottish whiskey-making tradition. In a way, that was our original intent. In our pursuit of an authentically American single malt whiskey, it brings our signature five-malt grain bill together with new American oak casks—two things practically unheard of in the old world. This combination produces a dramatically different whiskey from what is now commonplace and expected in the single malt category. But the goal wasn't simply to be different. Just as traditional styles of single malt from Scotland emerged as a reflection of regions such as Islay and Speyside, so too does our American Oak stay true to the provenance of our Pacific Northwest home.

"Undoubtedly, American Oak stands as our greatest departure from Scottish whiskey-making tradition."

In 2010, this was the idea. Could we summon the courage to look beyond the edges of whiskey as we knew it to create a single malt that honored tradition but also moved it forward in a new way? The intention was to create a balanced, grain-forward whiskey following the same basic processes used for generations in the old world, but the idea was bigger than that. We didn't want to simply replicate Scotch whisky in America. Instead, we wanted to create a whiskey that reflected the distinct qualities of the region we're from; of the place where it is made and character of those who make it. American Oak, or more precisely, its forebears, were the answer.

Let's be honest, in the beginning we were outliers in the industry at best. We'd had a few drams, read some issues of Whisky Magazine, and toured a handful of distilleries (or more). We were enthusiasts and students, but far from seasoned makers. But we had an idea and we simply started to chase it. American Oak is a whiskey with a lineage that includes products of different names, be it Mason Lake Malts, Deacon Seat, or simply Flagship. Before that, it was countless bottles in countless shapes with less creative names and notes scribbled across blue painter's tape. All of these iterations are manifestations of the same idea. All are important steps in the shaping of that idea that began ten years ago and continues

A PROVING GROUND

by Steve Hawley

Every story has a beginning. Westland's was set in an unassuming industrial park in south Seattle, Unit CE2. Enough years have now passed so that "CE2" is largely unfamiliar to all but a few at the distillery. It now stands as a short chapter in what is becoming a lengthy tale. But these humble beginnings should not be forgotten. It was here that the foundation of Westland was formed.

While this first distillery was short of a clandestine operation, CE2 was also far from a revolving door for the curious. We once considered stocking the bar we built for the "tasting room" but decided, rightfully so in hindsight, that our time was better spent heads down in the work of making whiskey. The bar instead became a staging site for quarterly tastings of our stocks and served as a more-than-serviceable coaster for our beers at day's end. With visions of lavish events and celebrations tucked away for the time being, we pressed forward in our pursuits.

Within those walls we cut our teeth in whiskey-making. Capacity at CE2 averaged about five casks a week (for reference, what we now typically fill in a day). While a few textbooks lined a wall of the "office", we learned by doing, which has become a habit we embrace to this day. We learned what to do, but more often what not to do. We deliberated on our ambitions, debated various approaches, refined our technique, and developed an intuitive feel for the nature of our house style. It was hard but rewarding work.

We're happy with the grand home we currently inhabit in the SoDo neighborhood of Seattle. Still, we look back on our time at CE2 fondly and gratefully, confident in the fact that we made more good choices than bad, and that all of them helped shape the Westland of today.

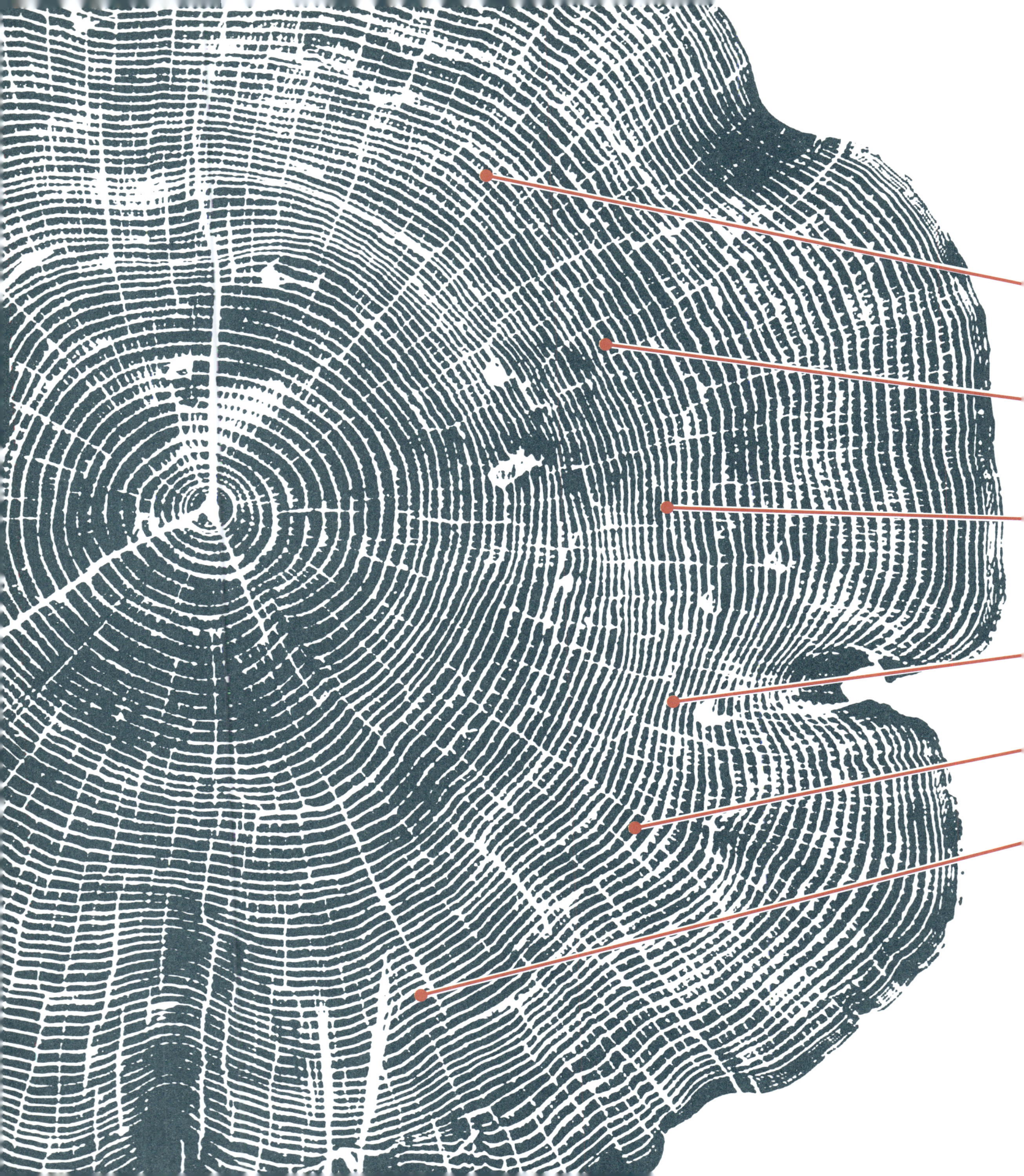

GROWING AMBITIONS

Early results, known only to a small group of us, were enough to swell our ambitions. Two more years of firsts were ahead of us, but we couldn't resist. Stagnancy was not an option. There was so much to explore and so much to imagine in single malt. We were still just getting started, but realized quickly that we needed a distillery suited to the opportunity and befitting our debut on the world stage.

1 JANUARY 2012: SODO DISTILLERY LEASE SIGNED
While Matt and team were busy at the task of filling five casks a week, Emerson was finalizing a deal to move into our current 13,000-square-foot home in the SoDo neighborhood of Seattle.

2 JULY 2012: THE GRAIN GATHERING
A seminal moment in the history of Westland when we first met Dr. Stephen Jones as well as the founders of Skagit Valley Malting. We began to see the future in barley while also narrowly averting a toiling path towards building our own malting plant.

3 OCTOBER 2012: NEW STILLS ARRIVAL
On a typically sunny fall Seattle day, our two new stills, made by Vendome Copper & Brass Works in Louisville, Kentucky, were quite literally swung into place. These would allow us to produce in a day what we could do in a week on our original Christian Carls.

4 MAY 2013: SODO DISTILLERY COMPLETE
Our new home, polished to a sparkling sheen, was fit for occupancy, and more importantly, the making of single malt whiskey.

5 OCTOBER 2013: DEACON SEAT RELEASE
With requisite aplomb, we welcomed friends and family through the doors of our new distillery for the first official Westland release of whiskey: Deacon Seat.

6 OCTOBER 2013: AMERICAN OAK LAUNCH
While it took several names in the early years as our portfolio evolved, American Oak, our first flagship single malt, made its debut in time to raise a toast for the holidays.

THE PROGRESS OF WESTLAND 2012–2013

55 | OUR WEST IS WHISKEY

THE PROMISE OF THE WEST | 58

PART THREE

RECONNECTING WHISKEY TO AGRICULTURE

"Nobody can discover the world for somebody else. Only when we discover it for ourselves does it become common ground and a common bond and we cease to be alone."

—

Wendell Berry

IN THE WORDS OF A FARMER

Learning about the land, from the people of that land, is a completely different experience from a lazy and impersonal Internet search. Through time spent together, in person, more than just essential information is passed on. In working with folks like Dave Hedlin, one of our key partners in Skagit Valley, we're gifted knowledge but also wisdom and inspiration. Our talks with Dave are filled with moments of wit that can disguise a depth of insight if you don't look closely enough. Below are a few of our favorite quotes from Dave.

"Ten years ago we grew grain for fun and occasional profit."

"There are only two good years in farming: 1918 and next year."

"Mother Nature never sleeps and she always bats last."

"In agriculture every success is temporary, every failure is permanent."

"We're all trying to gain a lifetime of golden eggs without having to trade it for one goose dinner."

"I know there's money in farming because we put it there."

"If I win a race to the bottom, then where am I?"

"I like 'optimist' so much better than 'stupid.'"

"The beautiful thing about a greenhouse is that you can control all the variables. The terrifying thing is that you have to."

"If we farmers are going to stay independent, we're going to have to work together."

"To call anything that we do 'sustainable' is the height of arrogance. What's important is to do the best we can do with the realities of the time and what we're given."

STEWARDING OUR LIVING HERITAGE

by Jack Algiere

Unpredictable moments of clarity arise out of the complex process of farming. It is enough to know these moments are waiting to be realized, like scattered puzzle pieces. Each new glimpse at the big picture somehow uncomplicates it. With these revelations comes an inexplicable feeling of accomplishment and growth as you recognize how our ecosystem, both wild and cultivated, fits together in such an intricate and complementary way. These are insights that have been lost or forgotten more so than they are new inventions. Farming with nature is full of these memories and glimpses of the ancient technology that allows this planet to thrive. Unfortunately, our common understanding of modern agriculture underestimates a greater set of values that can only be experienced through individual and personal connection. As it is with all forms of art—attention, practice, and humility are the ingredients that mature the knowledge.

To farm is to practice stewardship. I'd be remiss not to mention the sheer amount of food we produce, but in some ways, the abundance can be recognized as the result of good practice. In the most effective and supportive circumstances, 'farmer' is elevated beyond productionist and considered public and ecological servant as well. Good farming is culturally productive—a role that embraces the fundamental interdependence on ecosystem and society. At the core of a farmer's work is a call-and-response between people and their place that shapes our landscape as much as it seasons our cuisine. The finest artisanship has emerged from the most generative agricultural societies and vice versa. Each piece of food on a plate or whiskey in a bottle becomes an artifact of the story that reconnects us to the health and beauty of our place. Neglecting this relationship has untold repercussions to us and the planet. There are a handful of basic principles that are core to organic, regenerative, and sustainable agriculture. Above all, one stands out: nature adores diversity. Complex diversity matures with time and establishes balance and resilience. In this diversity, there are always mixed relationships of animals and plants, perennials and annuals. This is the work, nurturing these connections and cycles. We call it rotation in modern methodology, for animals and vegetables. Manure, compost, and plant roots are essential contributions to the soil biome. We strive for a self-generating, self-renewing system. The soil is the living foundation for health. Done properly, every piece of the puzzle finds its place, without waste. This is the great challenge.

"These are principles of nature that can be interpreted through practice."

These are principles of nature that can be interpreted through practice. If you're attentive, these biomimicry practices are easy to understand and highly adaptable to practical applications. Those applications are the extensions of agriculture. But to be fully productive, the same principles embraced by farmers must also extend to the cultures, cuisines, artforms, and experiences that follow. Each seed saved is a representation of a living heritage and a continuation of the agricultural tradition. It is our awareness and action as consumers and contributors that catalyzes the change in our food and farming culture for the better.

At an early age, farming offered me the right combination of ethics, skills, and inspiration, and that continues to ring true. Over the past two decades, I have had the great privilege to develop the diverse and innovative agro-ecological system at Stone Barns Center for Food & Agriculture in the lower Hudson Valley with the support of my family and a perceptive, adventurous network of chefs, artisans, craftsmen, and lovers of good food. My role has been to tend and cultivate this majestic landscape and to orchestrate a cultural experiment shaped by culinary and agricultural relationships. I have often recognized the rarity of our circumstance and work to reciprocate my gratitude by upholding the

"When we subdue our agricultural awareness, we lose our connections and relationship to the inspiration of the artform."

values of ecology and social equity through our work. With the help of an extraordinary team of young and talented farmers, we have shaped hundreds of acres of land in service to our ecosystem and a dialog with the community. In turn, we're providing the necessary and practical experience to confidently impact our food system.

I'm often asked if that impact comes at too great a cost. There is no doubt a cultural paradox that comes with the feeling of indulgence when buying an artisanal loaf, felted vest, handmade pottery, or handcrafted whiskey. Today, these are aspirational, and often expensive choices a consumer makes. But if we make a fundamental shift in mindset, focusing on keeping value where it's created and nurturing the relationship between place and people, we can make both more accessible and attainable. With each, the reverence and intention of the craft is an example of what we are attempting to restore in our culture. Agriculture and the master crafts that have emerged from its holistic complexity are one and the same. When we subdue our agricultural awareness, we lose our connections and relationship to the inspiration of the artform.

My friends at Westland know this story well. In a single glass of whiskey, the complexity of a whole cultural ecology is distilled into a simple amber spirit. The deeper you look, the richer the experience. The aesthetic of their craft expands beyond the mastered tradition to the subtleties of the grain and wood. It extends to the barley and the soil and to the oak and its savanna. Beyond that, it extends to the culture of the community and the stewardship of the ecosystem. Their dedication to transparency of process compels their team to innovate. This simple glass of whiskey is a fine example of the agricultural renaissance that is unfolding region by region and eye to eye.

My Scotch-Irish and Italian family has a long relationship with the land and a lasting whiskey tradition that stems from it. The celebratory ritual is a way to recall our ancestors and where we have come from. Each dram is an opportunity to look into each other's eyes in shared appreciation for the potency of the distilled moment. Well before I had a taste, the smell and the atmosphere of the experience had set in as a special and reverent moment. I surely give credit to my father and Papa for establishing this time-honored process in me. As the glasses make contact, so do we with each other and our culture. We say the names of our ancestors and with a simple "Salute," we pledge to uphold their loving memory.

Westland's commitment to developing unique quality and authenticity in each batch is a cultural inspiration as well as a finely crafted spirit. In the spirit of diversity, soil, and ecology, the process symbolizes a renewed awareness of the service that is embedded in each step from breeding to planting, from harvest to malting, and from mashing to barreling. And with it, a new revelation of how it can all fit together. Salute, to the time honored, to the process, to the distilled complexity, and to the reverence for harmony in craft and land.

BREEDING A REVOLUTION

by Steve Hawley

I first met Dr. Stephen Jones in the pages of *The Third Plate*, chef Dan Barber's remarkable manifesto on the future of food and the agricultural system that lies beneath it. The book has become required reading for all staff at Westland, not least of all because of the transformative profile of Dr. Jones in the book's final chapter. I've since come to know Dr. Jones personally and count him now as a good friend, even forgoing the formalities prescribed by his doctorate. He's just Steve to me now. As I am to him. But ironically, the more I come to know him, the more mythical a figure he becomes in my life.

Our partnership with Steve, The Bread Lab he directs, and a host of iconoclastic characters he's brought together in Skagit Valley has become a favorite chapter in the story of Westland. The work we do together to push the boundaries of provenance and barley exploration has become a shining symbol of what, fundamentally, the Westland pursuit is all about.

Without question Steve Jones is one of the preeminent grain breeders in the world, his focus and expertise being wheat, barley, and buckwheat. But his work in the Skagit Valley—for which he has attained celebrity status—began amidst trying circumstances. While working as a grain breeder at Washington State University in Pullman in Eastern Washington, Steve was asked to breed a proprietary strain of wheat for a corporate sponsor who would own the intellectual property. He refused. Under immense pressure to remove the man who stood in the way of this deal, Steve was exiled to a remote agricultural extension center in Burlington, Washington. No doubt they hoped he would fade quietly from the public stage. They obviously didn't know Steve Jones.

Banished from the commodity system and isolated from the rest of the agricultural community, he could've easily climbed into a shell and coasted to retirement. Instead, he became the central figure in one of the world's most dynamic agricultural systems and built a model for the future of grain.

Skagit Valley, and Steve's Bread Lab, sits about an hour north of Seattle (depending on who's driving) in one of the most fertile farming valleys in the world. Many there are fifth-generation farmers whose ancestors brought the same ambition and entrepreneurial spirit to the region that we so revere at Westland. They bought land with stumps on it and shaped it, instead of simply settling it. In the 80,000–acre valley I often hear farmers tell visitors that "the job of the Skagit River is to put the mountains to the east into the ocean to the west." Using methods brought from the old world, they built a system of dikes to stall that process and mitigate flooding, allowing them to harness the natural landscape and create a valley of incredible vitality, diversity, and bounty.

Not all regions have farmers with this vision and accompanying wherewithal. As Steve likes to say, "Here you can find people that say 'yes.'" The magic of the Skagit is found in the collective commitment to rotational farming. The practice of rotation keeps the soil healthy and leads to sustainable annual harvests that yield flavorful, nutritious, and valuable crops. This is also counter to the monocrop approach to agriculture that dominates most of the world's farming. Rotational farming is incredibly hard work that calls for cooperation, persistence, and a reliance on crops such as barley and wheat in order to be viable.

Grains are what make crop rotations work, returning vital organic matter back into the soil every few years on a given farm. The problem is, of the 80 different commercial crops grown in Skagit Valley, barley (sold at commodity prices) has historically been the least profitable. In fact, more often than not, farmers would lose money on the crop. As one of our growers Dave Hedlin says, "Ten years ago we grew grain for fun and occasional profit." This put a tremendous strain on farms financially, making it more challenging in recent years to stick with rotational farming while fending off the squeeze from two of the world's fastest-growing cities in Seattle and Vancouver, British Columbia, that would just as soon see it all paved. What Steve Jones ultimately recognized when he arrived to the Valley in 2009 was that, in order to preserve the Valley as farmland, the community needed to grow grains that had greater value. His mission was set.

Those who have been farming and stewarding the Valley for generations are quick to credit its newfound resilience and prosperity to Steve's progressive influence. In breeding grains of distinction, designed to prioritize flavor first and also succeed in Skagit Valley's unique terroir, he's triggered a paradigm shift in the entire system.

> *"Steve has a rare mix of acuity, imagination, humility, subversiveness, and conviction."*

There's no law in Skagit Valley (or most other regions for that matter) precluding different approaches. The agricultural system in America doesn't regulate new ideas out of the system. But prevailing convention absolutely stifles progress. The dogma that values efficiency and yield over time and flavor is firmly set. Liberating the Valley from the shackles of the commodity system itself, with a new grain economy benefitting the bottom line of the farmers and inspiring a fundamental shift in ideology, this is Steve's great achievement.

Steve has a rare mix of acuity, imagination, humility, subversiveness, and conviction. He carries it all with an unassuming quietness—one that, in his case, belies his stature in the world of agriculture. He's an easy man to talk to and it can often seem like you're simply shooting the breeze. But if you're an attentive student, you're served with a bewitching array of insight, inspiration, comedy, indignation, resolve, and faith.

Once you get to know Steve, you recognize that the weight of his own transcendence has taken its toll on him. His road has been a long one, with invigorating highs and frustrating lows. He'll be the first to admit that he's learned a great deal along the way that has shaped his perspective. He's not the type that wills himself to be right. He's open, honest. He acknowledges his own deliverances and unapologetically embraces evolution of thought. It all shows in his features and in his mannerisms, simultaneously buoyed and worn by it all.

Steve is a fountain of wisdom, usually packaged up in a collection of quotable one-liners that make you want to go write a book. For me, one adage always stands out from the rest, "We need to add time back in as an ingredient." He believes efficiency at any cost is something we should reject. He believes time adds flavor and value. When faced with the pressure of urgency, he implores us always to be critical by asking the question, "Who does it truly benefit?" This underscores who Steve is, or better put, who he has become. I'm painting a picture of this Zen-like master but in choosing to step away from commodity and convention Steve actually takes on an even greater responsibility that would be challenging for any of us to burden. Putting yourself out of place, away from the grain belt of America and its influences, can be insolating and stressful. At The Bread Lab though, amongst the company of kindred spirits that turnstile in and out of his door like the Frozen ride at Disneyland, he's found a peace. Make no mistake, Steve's version of peace isn't stillness. Far from it. He wakes on farmer time (whatever ungodly hour that is) and is still unequivocally restless at heart. But in today's world of instant gratification, he doesn't need the quick answer. He's patient, letting those answers reveal themselves when ready. He is loyal to the process and works with the truths and pace of nature, not against them. He'll never be able to shake his relentless curiosity but now that curiosity comes with less imposed pressure to prove anything to anyone. His lone looming albatross is securing and advancing an inquiry that first began over a century ago, which he dutifully and gratefully accepts even in the face of a dismissive establishment.

Over a thousand words in now and I haven't even begun to mine the depths of our partnership with Steve, The Bread Lab, and Skagit Valley more broadly. There is so much to tell, and we'll do so in the months and years to come, in both words and whiskey. Alongside us will be Dr. Steve Jones, the wise sage reminding us that what we're doing is not only innovative, but inherently valuable on a scale that goes well beyond whiskey.

THE PACIFIC NORTHWEST

1. WESTLAND DISTILLERY
Our distillery and tasting room are located in the heart of Seattle's industrial SoDo district.

2. SKAGIT VALLEY
Here we work with breeders, growers, and maltsters to develop unique varieties of barley for our whiskey.

3. SHELTON PEAT BOG
One of many bogs in the state, we're working with partners to harvest local peat.

4. PALOUSE REGION
The majority of our barley is sourced from this region of the state and is certified Grown in Washington.

5. GARRY OAK SAVANNAS
In a 50-mile-wide band up the I-5 corridor from Northern California to Southern British Columbia, we find native oak to use for our Garryana whiskey.

PLANTING A NEW SEED

by Steve Hawley

If there's anything we've become known for over our first ten years, it's our indignation over the whiskey industry's disregard for barley. We've been outspoken and have undoubtedly ruffled a few feathers. But it's important to prompt the debate. Single malt whiskey, globally, is at an important crossroads. While whiskey has humble roots as an agricultural product that was made and consumed near its source, industrialization and globalization gave rise to a new model where stocks of spirit were distilled at the lowest price, then bought and sold on the open market for blends. Malt whiskey became a commodity and along the way something meaningful was lost. But now we live in times where once again single malt is revered and we can make choices based on new standards. In today's world, we can confidently step away from the commodity mindset and return to a reverence for raw materials and a pursuit of flavor.

As one of just four ingredients in single malt, it's surprising to see that the vast majority of whiskey makers have yet to really imagine what more barley can give us. This is largely due to the still swift current of economic motive—the proverbial race to the bottom. Certainly this has, in part, encouraged the pervasive dogma that barley doesn't contribute to flavor in whiskey. But the truth is, many who adhere to this prevailing wisdom do so because they've never known anything different. The global barley breeding community develops varieties of barley to suit the demands of the industry and the system. Those demands are, (a) strong disease resistance, (b) high yields for the farmer and within the distillery, and (c) a grain that malts consistently and successfully within the macro-malt system. Admirable goals, all of them. But what's conspicuously missing is flavor. Breeders are giving the malting and distilling industry exactly what they're asking for, and as a result, whiskey makers are left with barleys that are all but exactly the same in character. As the whiskey industry has become increasingly married to the commodity system, the notion that barley actually matters has faded from their collective mind.

When we first started in 2010, the idea that barley is simply a means to an end (that end being solely the collection of alcohol) didn't sit right. What if we elevated the role of barley in whiskey? What if we could breed barleys with flavor first in mind? After several futile years attempting to convince suppliers to step with us beyond the commodity system, we resolved to build it ourselves, and in 2012, a door opened for us that would change the course of Westland forever. In the town of Burlington, Washington, an hour north of Seattle, we met the good folks at The Bread Lab and Skagit Valley Malting who in turn introduced us to several of the Valley's most progressive farmers. In two years of buying barley in Washington State and beyond, we hadn't once met a grower. In fact, we were forbidden from doing so by our existing suppliers. Now we had the opportunity to collaborate with everyone in the chain—from breeding to growing, malting to distilling.

Everyone in the room recognized that if we stopped treating barley like a commodity and instead consider it thoughtfully as the main raw ingredient and a source of flavor in single malt whiskey, it promised a world of benefit for everyone involved. So, we set out together to build an entirely new economy for barley and a proving ground for new ideas. Since those first days our work has been an ever-expanding inquiry into the infinite possibilities to be found in barley.

Today, we are on the outer edges of knowledge and the brink of an exponential leap forward not only for our own industry, but also for our regional agricultural community at large. The compass by which we navigate now is a new fellowship program that Westland is fully funding at The Bread Lab. With access to the Lab's seed bank, which houses thousands of different varieties of barley dating back centuries, the program is dedicated to developing novel barleys for whiskey. The charter of the fellowship is to research and breed barleys that fall outside the commodity system while balancing three primary objectives:

RECONNECTING WHISKEY TO AGRICULTURE | 86

First, the barley must work for the farmer. For too long, growers in this country have been left behind, squeezed by the cruel machinations of industrialization and commodification. We don't view ourselves as simply end users for barley. We see Westland as an integral part of a community and an agricultural system that betters the land and its people. Our role in that community is not to drive people down, as is the capitalistic norm, but to help build everyone up. We must create value for each and every person in the system, starting with the farmer. This means that the varieties we develop must be grown in an economically viable way that provides meaningful income for the grower. That means both yield and value (read: novelty and flavor). Equally as important, the varieties must be suitable to a role in farming, not just whiskey. Each new variety must help sustain complete crop rotations so growers can improve their soil and perpetuate a healthy agricultural system.

"We see Westland as an integral part of a community and an agricultural system that betters the land and its people."

Second, the barley must work for the changing environment. In just the past decade the rate of change in our climate and ecosystems has accelerated to the point of outright unpredictability. We are not spared from these forces, even in the relatively isolated and idyllic Pacific Northwest. The preservation of healthy farmland requires both economic and ecological alacrity. In addition to aiding in rotational farming, the varieties we develop in the fellowship program must be suited to certified organic, regenerative organic, Salmon-Safe, or other low-impact cultivation methods. But beyond stewardship of the land as it exists, we must also be prepared for what it might become. We breed with the unknown in mind, bringing back genetic diversity to barley, and judging the success of a variety partly on its ability to withstand (or tolerate) changes wrought by global climate change.

Finally, the barley must work for the end consumer. This should be obvious. Even if it checks each and every other box, if it isn't delicious, it's not worth pursuing. In fact, we take it one step further. If it isn't good *and* unique, it's not worth pursuing. Uniqueness and novelty are not things to be feared, but rather embraced. We breed varieties for these qualities because, in the end, if it tastes like everything else, what's the point?

Our first PhD student in the fellowship program, Louie Prager, began his work in 2020. He is the first in what we hope will be a long line of researchers to carry forward this ambition. It's fascinating to witness Louie, a bakery owner and biologist who carries none of the baggage that we do from the world of whiskey, create his own relationship to the inquiry. At first, he was simply gaining a basic understanding of technique, history, environment. But quickly his work has become more a communion with the barley. A slow, incremental awakening is unfolding. It's intensely personal. He describes his work as a dance and his job to find a rhythm within it.

It is this level of familiarity that will greatly benefit everyone that follows in the chain, from farmer to maltster to distiller. For Westland, the fellowship is a long-term proposition, one we invest the whole of ourselves into. This is the only way in which it can be successful. This isn't something any of us can be detached from if it's to work in the end. Only when you get this intimate with a process can you find the opportunities within it.

The relationship to barley that we're cultivating—both individually and collectively—is so far removed from the rote barley ordered with a click of a button on the commodity market. In just ten short years we have already distilled over 20 different varieties of barley, each with a character distinct from the other. We've proven that barley can not only contribute to flavor in whiskey, it can also define it. We've made our choice at the crossroads, but have only just begun to imagine where it might lead. One thing we know for sure: it'll be way more rewarding than the short road to uniformity.

THE HUNT FOR GARRY OAK

by Matt Hofmann

In the spring of 2017, we thundered down Interstate 5 in a torrent of rain, something none will find surprising. We were up early and we were alert, thanks to a few gallons of coffee, a stiff mid-winter wind and the excitement of the chase. If I'm being honest, we were feeling part excitement and part nervous anticipation. We had a lot riding on this trip to Southern Oregon. Untold potential waited ahead—or perhaps more accurately, unseen potential.

Whiskey teaches you many things, not the least of which is perspective. I've become practiced at mentally removing myself from the moment. Never entirely, but in small bits. I'm still easily caught up in the doing of things, but I've also learned how important it is to be continually aware of the bigger picture. We've long seen new possibilities in single malt whiskey and with each step forward we recognize how our work impacts our place in the industry. We don't take this lightly. And so, we make a study of understanding both the business and the craft of whiskey. Without attention to both you can't succeed at either. When we pause to step outside the moment, the picture can develop. What comes into focus is everything that has come and gone, and that which has yet to come. The pattern and machinations of our actions appear fluid, almost predictable. One can't help but smile at the beauty of the work we have the fortune to pursue, of the influences from the past balanced against the thrilling path we see in the future.

On this day, we were hunting for Garry Oak (*Quercus garryana*), the native oak species that only grows here in the Pacific Northwest. While we've been filling casks made from this remarkable wood for several years and making unique and delicious whiskeys with it, we've always acknowledged how lucky we've been thus far. Just the year prior we found a cache of cut lumber that gave us enough raw material for the 25 casks we made and filled during that summer. Some of that lumber had air-dried for three years. Some for five years. And some, even for seven years. This was the proverbial goldmine. Thousands of board feet of perfectly-seasoned Garry Oak, ready to go. But we're not ones to rely on luck time and time again, and our ambitions were growing.

Based on the results of our early work with Garry Oak, we're investing more and more into the species. But now we are confronted with the reality of the present. Because this oak is so rare and so difficult to find, no system has been built for it. With our plans expanding to 50 casks a year, we now need a minimum of 10,000 board feet of Garry Oak per year. So, we had to architect the system and create the economy. That began by developing relationships close to the source so we can be alerted to any raw oak that becomes available. Looking out the window of the truck, we knew those sources were out there ahead of us, if we looked hard enough.

Garry Oak has long been an afterthought in this region. Today, it is still largely seen as scrap by most, used for firewood if anything at all. It's used only sparingly for industry—flooring, furniture and, of course, whiskey—though it is seeing a small resurgence. In the face of that renewed interest however, is a stark reality. Garry Oak now grows only in roughly five percent of its former habitat. Being found in some of the most coveted grazing areas when early pioneers first moved into the region, it came down quickly to make way for homesteads and settlements. Only recently have preservation efforts been undertaken to maintain and restore these special habitats that had once been looked after by Native Americans for millennia. Many local and regional authorities have now put restrictions

> *"Being found in some of the most coveted grazing areas when early pioneers first moved into the region, it came down quickly to make way for homesteads and settlements."*

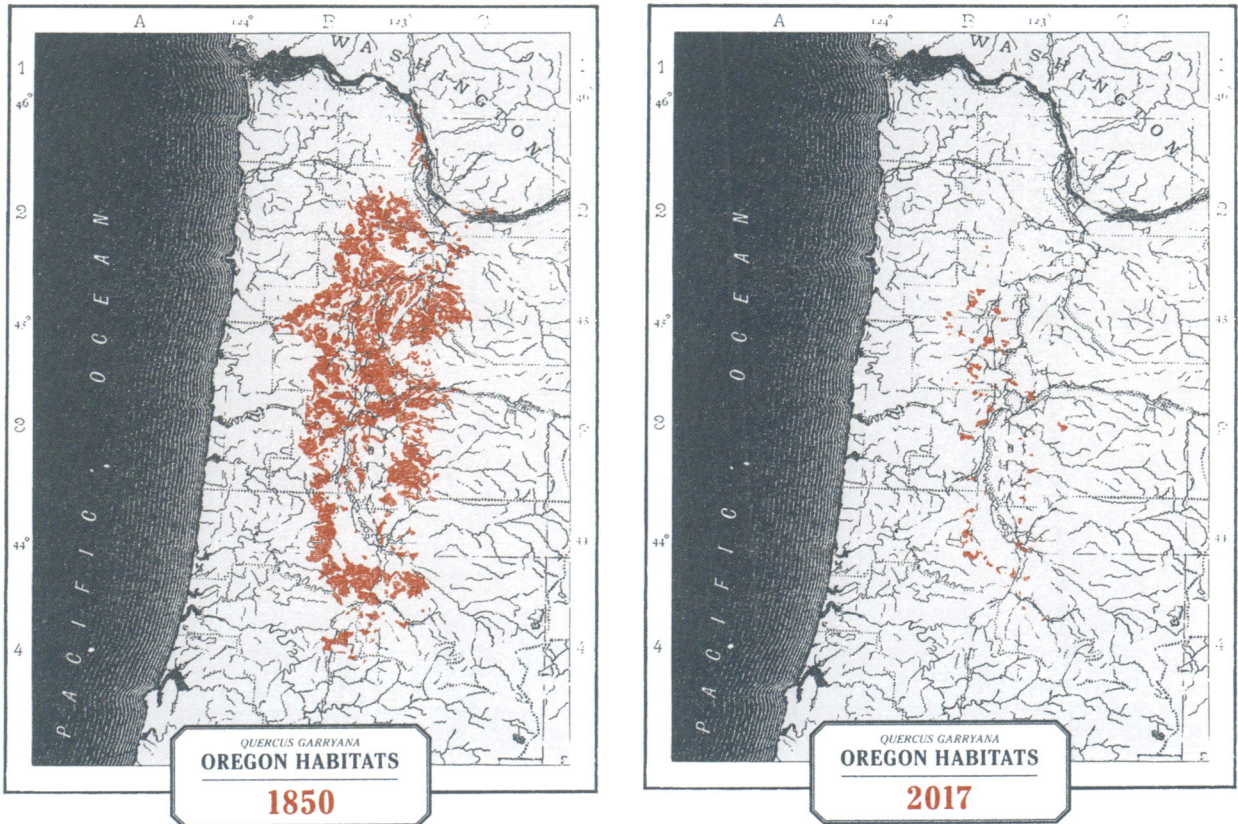

QUERCUS GARRYANA
OREGON HABITATS
1850

QUERCUS GARRYANA
OREGON HABITATS
2017

into place for bringing down Garry Oak. Unfortunately, during the era when these oak savannas were neglected, a large lumber industry focused on planting and harvesting coniferous trees was established. What we're left with now is a once-revered species of oak that has been marginalized by the advance of society. As a result, usable Garry Oak, blown down in storms or secured from one of the few remaining pockets of legal urban salvage, is now extremely rare.

It's no surprise then that a substantial cooperage economy has yet to take root in this region. When we source *Quercus alba*, commonly known as American White Oak, we work within a large coopering system that allows us to source what we want, when we want it, with a simple phone call or click of the mouse. We have demanding specifications relative to the rest of the whiskey industry, particularly in our search for air-dried oak. But even those self-imposed restrictions don't cause a great challenge when dealing with *Quercus alba*. For the coopers who supply us with those casks—who do a fantastic job by the way—the stock of raw oak is widely available. With Garry Oak, however, when we want 100 casks, made from three-year air-dried wood, our fortunes are left only to chance and timing.

> "It was apparent that we needed to secure wood now—not just for this year's demand, but for years to come. That meant finding 50,000 board feet."

Reminded of all of these factors, we realized the enormity of the task. It was apparent that we needed to secure wood now—not just for this year's demand, but for years to come. That meant finding 50,000 board feet. Rather than breaking our spirit though, we found resolve. We pulled off I-5 near Halsey, Oregon, where we'd learned of a small family farm that might prove fruitful. This was no hipster farm; this is real, rural America, a picture that could have been taken in any one of a thousand places in the US, save for the oaks. We met Samuel Kropf and his son Norman, who cut oak from their property on a small Lucas mill with a circular saw. Though we would only source 1,000 board feet on this day, we developed a relationship that promised a steady albeit relatively small supply for years to come. No matter how much you know or care about whiskey, coopering, or even oak itself, there was a bigger idea taking shape starting with that first visit. There is great and often unappreciated value to be found in what literally lies all around us. To find new uses for this wood and to provide a new source of revenue to the salt-of-the-earth farming families of the region is a remarkable sea change for what is a growing community of like-minded people we're bringing together.

I often see a lot of corollaries between the world of whiskey-making and the world of food. One of the problems with our modern agricultural system is that people don't tend to have much of a connection to where the food they eat comes from. They can't see the nuances of what went into raising these particular vegetables or what was fed to the chicken they're going to roast for dinner. But when people make it out to a farm and see everything the farmer must do to get those vegetables through the season or that chicken to a full size, they tend to appreciate the food they're eating more than they would otherwise. So it is with oak. Once we saw the lumber yard at Goby Walnut Products and listened to them talk about their work, we really began to get a sense of what it takes to deliver the final lumber we'll use for casks and the pride they take in their workmanship.

We learned how challenging it is to source the raw oak, discussing the nuances of tree selection and exactly how it should be brought down. We listened to them wax poetic about the ways oak can be cut to varying thicknesses, say 4/4 or 5/4, depending upon the intended use. We heard about exactly what would happen to the oak if it were cut one way or the other. Listening to all of this was fascinating and immensely valuable to us as we considered how to work with the oak downstream. But perhaps the most interesting moment of the day didn't even concern oak at all, at least not yet.

There were walnut slabs there at the mill, ranging in size from simply large to incredibly massive. However, the thing that caught my eye was not the size of the slabs but the color. Ranging from caramel brown to shades of red, black, even purple and blue, the color of the wood reflected the growing conditions and the soil makeup from where the tree grew. As I was talking to the folks at Goby about this, we all realized the potential of what we had seen: if the different soil conditions could produce different colors in the tree, certainly it could be doing different things to flavor compounds and their precursors in the wood.

The ramifications weren't lost on any of us. Within minutes, we all got it. This is what we were there to do, establish a system for sourcing, milling and coopering—and form real relationships with real people. By building this economy from the ground up, we now not only have a more steady supply of oak, but we are able to control exactly how it is handled throughout the process.

We left Goby's mill in Portland to hunt down a few more leads. As we did, it felt as if everything fit so precisely in a nexus of time. Our continued work to create whiskeys that are real, that have a sense of time and place, to find the truth in our world and explore it, stirred a sense of purpose within all of us. The broader perspective was coming back into focus. The cycle is always self-reinforcing. We look "west," seeing the possibilities therein, then we push forward to make it so. We do this out of necessity and we know others will follow. Yet the heavy lifting and the difficulty that comes with carving the path also means we get to determine where it leads.

This has always been at the heart of our philosophy at Westland, ingrained in our very nature. We're compelled to look out so we might see possibilities others don't recognize. But seeing opportunity is not enough. You have to have the wherewithal to do something about it. During that trip, we explored one of the few remaining natural Garry Oak savannas in the Pacific Northwest. It was coated with lush mosses draping the otherwise bare limbs in the middle of winter. The oaks provided a juxtaposition of a life frozen in time and a world moving steadily forward. Again, we removed ourselves from the moment, wondering in amazement at our place in the world of whiskey, exploring physically at the edge of the earth and figuratively at the cutting edge of single malt philosophy. We, like our whiskeys, are products of our time and place. While we look forward to the future we're building with our new partners in this industry, we cannot deny that what we live for now in the present is the exploration, the journey. Each edition of Garryana is another step forward along a path that winds all across the Pacific Northwest in search of insight. We hope you enjoy the results as much as we do.

POSSIBILITY IN VARIETY

by Tyler Pederson

Over the past ten years, we've been fortunate enough to distill dozens of varieties of barley. Some of them have impressive pedigrees and extensive historical use in the brewing and distilling industries. Many others, however, have been non-traditional malting varieties that would normally end up as food for humans or livestock. Working with so many unique varieties of barley is an interesting opportunity that has been born out of necessity. Our approach to whiskey-making has always been to highlight the flavors of our raw ingredients. So, it was very surprising to learn that most everyone in the Scotch whisky industry was ignoring the flavor contributions of malted barley. Traditional breeding programs are pressured to select for varieties that can adapt to a broad geographic range and produce high yields. Farmers then have the interesting challenge of balancing their farming practices to harvest "malt grade" barley while still obtaining reasonable yields. If a harvest is out of spec due to an over application of nitrogen fertilizer, the farmer could end up with a near-worthless "feed grade" barley crop. Given the many financial pitfalls before them, barley farmers are too often compelled to plant common varieties from approved lists, resulting in uniform crops with no noteworthy flavors.

Realizing how flawed the traditional system was, we began working in earnest to build a new grain economy from scratch. We reached out to local research institutions, farmers, and craft malt houses to develop a grain economy that is resilient to the winds of change, while also being nimble enough to adapt to the changing needs of its partners. We seek out highly flavorful varieties that are locally adapted for our region. If we can't find a variety that makes great whiskey and works for everyone in the system, we move on to the next one. There are thousands of varieties out there for us to work with. It's an incredibly rewarding endeavor that has been yielding some incredibly delicious results!

ALBA

ROWS: 6-Row

SEASON: Winter

BREEDER: OSU/WSU

BREEDING YEAR: 1997

This 6-row winter variety is the progeny of the varieties Strider and Orca. Developed by Dr. Pat Hayes at Oregon State University, this variety was co-selected for the Skagit Valley in conjunction with Washington State University's The Bread Lab and registered in 2014. While initially released for the animal feed market, early trials showed malting potential as well. This was the first batch of malt that Westland received from Skagit Valley Malting (SVM), and the yields were surprisingly higher than the conventional malting variety (CDC Copeland) that we distilled the following week. The spirit quality is fantastic, and we are excited to be sharing it in our inaugural release of Colere.

BERE

ROWS: 6-Row

SEASON: Spring

BREEDER: Unknown

BREEDING YEAR: Unknown

Bere is an heirloom grain and one of the very first varieties that distillers used to make whiskey in Scotland. This 6-row spring variety can be difficult to work with due to its high levels of proteins and beta-glucans. A keen attention to the mill settings and mashing procedure is required to make a proper whiskey with this generally low-yielding barley. Husk and bran aromas are quite noticeable.

BARONESSE

ROWS: 2-Row

SEASON: Spring

BREEDER: Nordsaat, Germany

BREEDING YEAR: 1980s

Released in Germany during the 1980s, this 2-row spring variety struggled to find success in the malt market. It was then rebranded as a feed variety and became one of the most popular varieties in the Northwest during the 1990s. The rights to the seed have since changed hands several times, and now Bill Meyers of Joseph's Grainery in the Palouse is the sole farmer of this grain. Malted by LINC Malt, this variety has tons of biscuit flavor.

CDC BOW

ROWS: 2-Row

SEASON: Spring

BREEDER: Crop Development Center, Canada

BREEDING YEAR: 2005

Taking its name from the Bow River, this is a new 2-row spring variety released from the Crop Development Center in Canada. This low protein malt has been an efficient and high-yielding variety for our mash house and stillroom. It produces a very clean distillate.

CDC FRASER

ROWS: 2-Row

SEASON: Spring

BREEDER: Crop Development Center, Canada

BREEDING YEAR: 2016

Registered in 2016 and named after the Fraser River in British Columbia, this variety has agronomic yields slightly better than Bow, but is not as resistant to lodging. We used this variety for the first time in 2020 as a peated malt and have really enjoyed it as a vehicle for translating the rich phenolics of the bog.

CONCERTO

ROWS: 2-Row

SEASON: Spring

BREEDER: LG Seeds Company

BREEDING YEAR: 2006

Registered in 2006, this is a 2-row spring variety that has been one of the most popular varieties of malt for the UK distilling industry over the last decade. This malt has great yields for farmers and distillers alike. It makes a pleasant new make spirit, although not one of remarkable complexity.

LCS CALYPSO

ROWS: 2-Row

SEASON: Winter

BREEDER: Limagrain Cereal Seeds, UK

BREEDING YEAR: 2015

A variety with Maris Otter in its pedigree, this 2-row winter variety is a strong grower in maritime climates and yields a grain with low levels of beta-glucans. High levels of beta-glucans can increase the viscosity of our wort, making the lautering process increasingly difficult.

FRANCIN

ROWS: 2-Row

SEASON: Spring

BREEDER: Selgen

BREEDING YEAR: 2014

The story goes that this variety is the same that is used to make a certain popular beer from the Czech Republic. The rights to the grow seed were secured by chance while a couple of Pacific Northwest farmers were having beers in a European tavern. The distillate made from this pale malt has aromas full of citrus, custard, and phyllo dough. When it is peated, an aroma of smoky crème brûlée can be found in the new make spirit.

FRITZ (NZ151)

ROWS: 2-Row

SEASON: Spring

BREEDER: WSU

BREEDING YEAR: 2014

With Baronesse in its pedigree, this 2-row spring variety was co-developed by the Washington State University barley breeding program and Dr. Stephen Jones at The Bread Lab. Testing has shown strong agronomic performance on both sides of the Cascade Range. The generally higher protein content means that this variety is likely destined for the feed market as well. The malt makes an interesting new make spirit with lots of tropical fruit character underlined by notes of fried dough.

LCS GENIE

ROWS: 2-Row

SEASON: Spring

BREEDER: Limagrain Cereal Seeds, UK

BREEDING YEAR: 2013

First registered in 2015, this variety is adapted to grow well over a broad range of locations. This malted barley generally has low beta-glucan levels and good yields. It has become a favorite of many of our Salmon-Safe certified growers.

FULL PINT

ROWS: 2-Row

SEASON: Spring

BREEDER: OSU

BREEDING YEAR: 2014

The progeny of the Orca and Harrington varieties, this 2-row spring variety was first bred by Oregon State University in 2014. This variety grows better in Oregon than it does in Washington, so when it is available to us we get really excited for the rich, bready malt character that comes through in the distillate.

GOLDEN PROMISE

ROWS: 2-Row

SEASON: Spring

BREEDER: Miln Marsters Breeding Company

BREEDING YEAR: 1964

This is a seminal barley variety in the world of whiskey production. It was created in the UK in 1964 by inducing a mutation in the cultivar Maythorpe through the application of gamma ray radiation. Not only has this variety been prized for its assistance in the study of barley genetics, its use by brewers and distillers made it one of the most popular varieties in the UK from 1968-1990. In recent decades it has fallen out of favor as distillers have increasingly turned to higher-yielding varieties, but Golden Promise has a classic flavor that is still cherished to this day.

LYON

ROWS: 2-Row

SEASON: Spring

BREEDER: WSU

BREEDING YEAR: 2014

This variety of barley was bred by Kevin Murphy's breeding program at Washington State University to give the farmers of the Palouse a high-yielding crop that they could fit into their crop rotations. This descendent of Baronesse is a 2-row spring variety with specifications that would normally send this to the feed market. Brave maltsters in the craft sector are proving that it can make great quality malt as well. From a distiller's perspective it has been fairly easy to mash and distill, with aromas of baked goods and dried fruits in the new make spirit.

LCS ODYSSEY

ROWS: 2-Row

SEASON: Spring

BREEDER: Limagrain Cereal Seeds, UK

BREEDING YEAR: 2011

The progeny of the varieties Quench and Concerto, this is a high-yielding 2-row spring variety that was first bred in 2011. This variety has been really nice to work with and the new make spirit has aromas of baking spices, dried apples, and breakfast pastries.

MARIS OTTER

ROWS: 2-Row

SEASON: Winter

BREEDER: UK Plant Breeding Institute, Cambridge

BREEDING YEAR: 1965

This variety was first bred in 1965 and quickly became the most popular variety in the UK malt whisky industry for a time. The offspring of the varieties Pioneer and Proctor, this 2-row winter variety is prized for its noticeable "malty" flavor. It has since become the focus of many researchers and barley breeders who are looking to develop varieties for improved flavor characteristics.

OBSIDIAN

ROWS: 2-Row

SEASON: Spring

BREEDER: WSU

BREEDING YEAR: Unknown

Obsidian is a group of purple, hull-less, 2-row spring varieties of barley that are malted by Skagit Valley Malting. These varieties trace their historical and genetic roots back to Egypt as well as the Himalayas. With high levels of beta-glucan and a lack of a hull, these varieties are optimal for consumption as food by people. As whiskey makers though, those two properties make it an extremely challenging raw ingredient for us to work with. We must augment our mashing and lautering procedures to accommodate for these unique malts, but the delicious and complex nutty character of the new make spirit make it worth the effort.

PILOT

ROWS: 2-Row

SEASON: Spring

BREEDER: WSU

BREEDING YEAR: Unknown

This 2-row spring variety caught the eye of a local maltster during the breeding trials and its development has been a pleasant surprise in our line-up of malt varieties. It generally yields well, and the pale malt produces a very clean distillate. As a peated malt, it takes up all of that smoke and translates the aromas of the bog quite nicely.

WINTMALT

ROWS: 2-Row

SEASON: Winter

BREEDER: KWS Lochow, Germany

BREEDING YEAR: 2005

As the name suggests, this is a 2-row winter variety of barley. A descendant of Maris Otter, this has good malting potential and is a great option for growers looking for disease resistance. It's currently the most widely grown winter variety of malting barley in the Pacific Northwest. The new make spirit is complex and has aromas of breakfast cereal, honey, stewed berries, and floral notes.

TALISMAN

ROWS: 2-Row

SEASON: Winter

BREEDER: Senova

BREEDING YEAR: Unknown

Talisman is a variety that made a brief splash with brewers in the UK after it was first registered in 2012. This 2-row winter variety has Maris Otter in its pedigree and has some great biscuity flavors as a result.

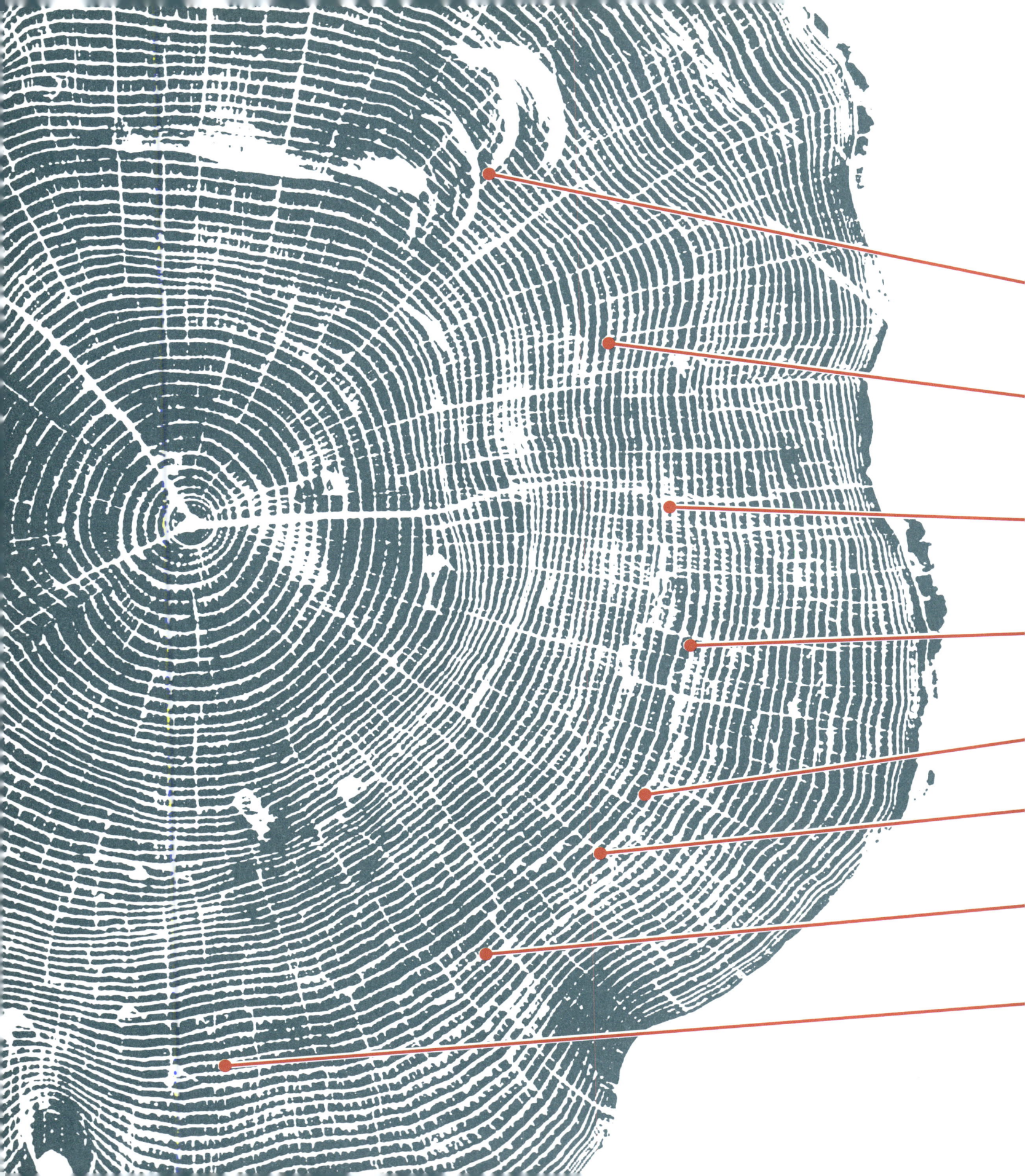

FILLING OUR SHOES (WITH WHISKEYS)

THE PROGRESS OF WESTLAND 2014–2015

As we hit our stride, the core tenets of Westland began to take full shape with the completion of our trinity of single malts and a growing recognition across the industry. These years were filled with ideas like the previous years, but now also with new whiskeys. The reception was both humbling and exhilarating. It was working, but a taste of early success only served to fuel our resolve to push further.

1 FEBRUARY 2014: FIRST PEATED RELEASE
One of our first loves, peated whiskey, was finally filled into bottles with this rare and limited release. It brought with it yet another American interpretation of an age-old tradition and established Westland's penchant for unabashedly simple naming.

2 JULY 2014: INAUGURAL PEAT WEEK FESTIVAL
So consumed with our forays into peat, we decided to replicate old world whiskey festivals right here in Seattle. Peated whiskey in July with sprinklers? Sounded like a good idea at the time.

3 NOVEMBER 2014: PEATED RELEASE
Our vision for Westland's portfolio was becoming clearer by the day, driven by our interests and our fans' not-so-subtle demands. A regular peated single malt was atop their list.

4 DECEMBER 2014: SHERRY WOOD RELEASE
To complete the trinity and our Core Range, Sherry Wood offered yet another new world perspective on old world traditions.

5 MARCH 2015: SF WORLD SPIRITS COMPETITION CRAFT WHISKEY OF THE YEAR
This was the first indication from a globally renowned whiskey competition that Westland was on the right path.

6 JUNE 2015: SECOND HOQUIAM RACKHOUSE
When we first started, we had the luxury of occupying an existing building in Hoquiam, Washington, to house our growing stocks of maturing whiskey. By summer of 2015, we had already outgrown that space.

7 OCTOBER 2015: BREAD LAB SPONSORSHIP BEGINS
As our belief in the possibilities for flavor in barley grew, so did our commitment to our oldest partner in the pursuit, WSU's The Bread Lab. Since 2015 we've helped support their critical work each year.

8 NOVEMBER 2015: ALBA VARIETY DISTILLATION
A seminal moment in the history of Westland and the whiskey industry, we distilled our first batch of malt made from a variety of barley bred for flavor and novelty first and grown outside the commodity system.

THE WEEK OF REEK

by Steve Hawley

Our intention with Westland has never been to turn our backs on tradition completely. In fact, we are first and foremost ardent lovers of single malt whiskey in all its many forms, always have been. We too were once charmed by the conventions of the old world and we want to carry forward those customs that we admire, even while interpreting them in our own unique ways. We've long revered two traditions in particular—peated whiskeys and whiskey festivals. With our annual Peat Week celebrations, we honor both.

Peated single malt, the oldest style of whiskey, has always held a special place in our hearts. It's what drew us to the métier in the first place. It's a constant whisper in our ear even when we're focused on other ideas. So, each year we set everything else aside for a week to inhabit peat fully, in whiskey and in ceremony. With Peat Week, we recreate our own version of time-honored traditions here in the Pacific Northwest.

Our Peat Week bottlings have received widespread critical acclaim at competitions the world over. Our weeklong celebration has become one of the most anticipated events of the year at the distillery. And the circus theme? Our fans have come to love the show of it all. We present these bottlings in a different light intentionally. Since the heavily peated whiskeys we bottle for Peat Week diverge from our typical house style, so too should their dressings be distinct. The ballyhoo is a welcome reprieve for our team and a fun way for our fans to build their own relationship with the wonders of peat. As we often say, "Step right up! The Week of Reek is here but once a year!"

RECONNECTING WHISKEY TO AGRICULTURE | 110

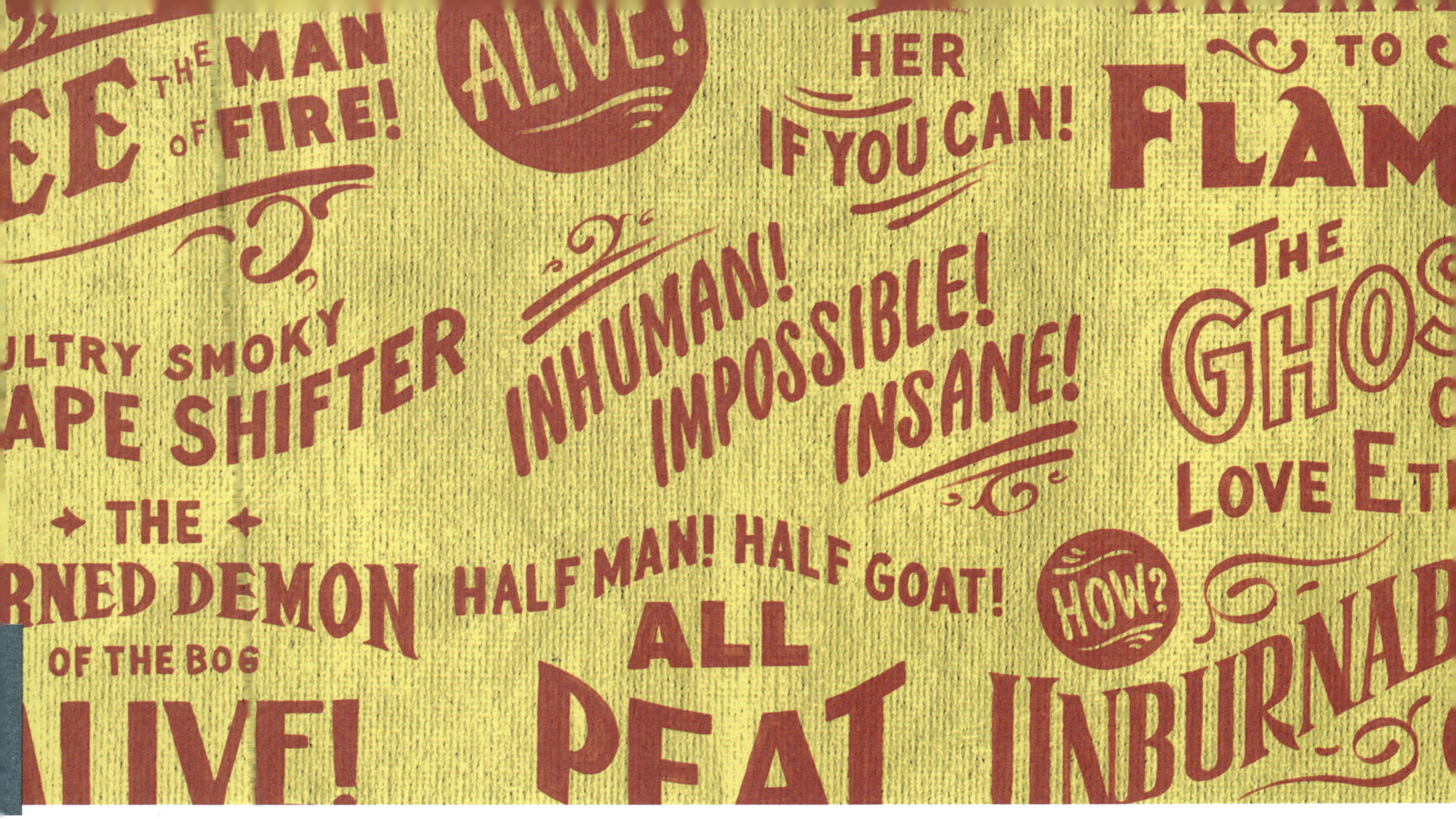

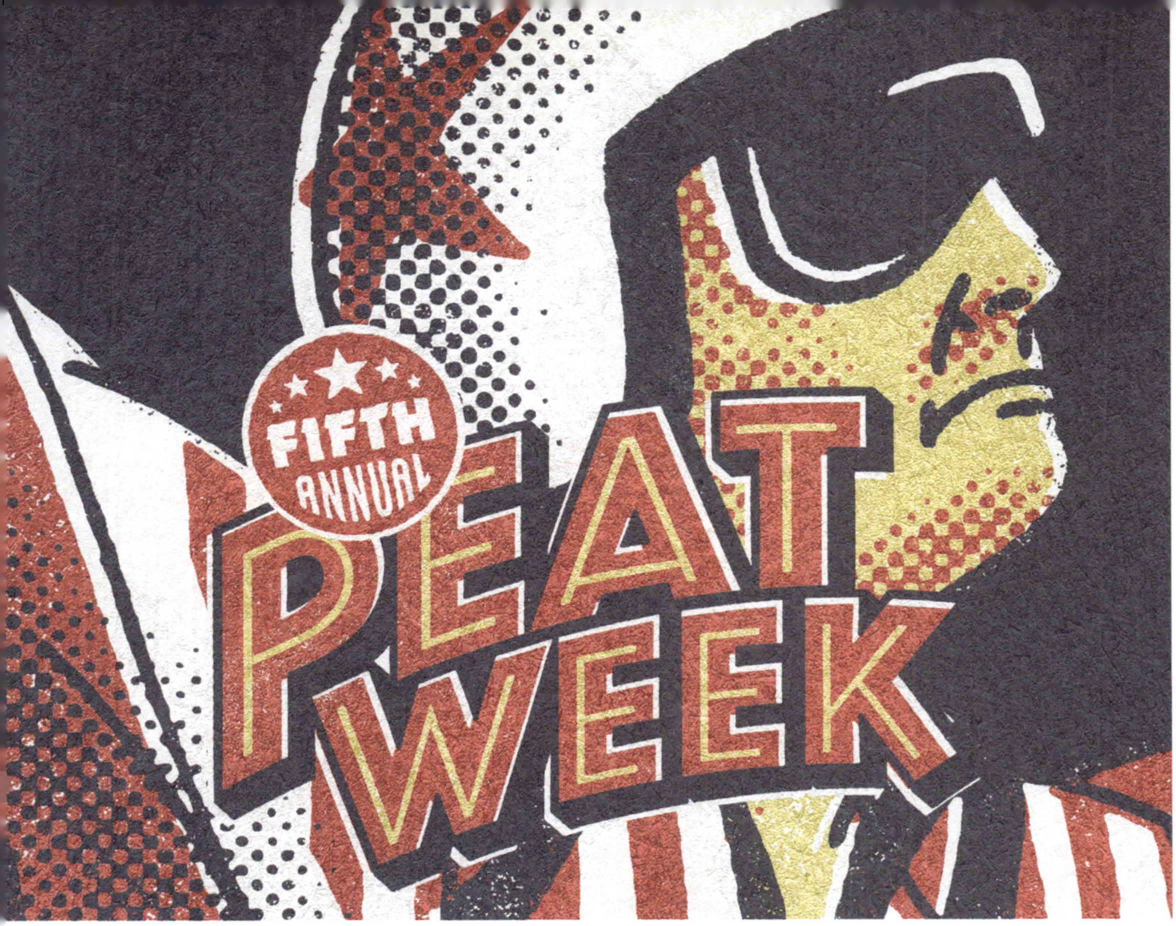
FIFTH ANNUAL
PEAT WEEK

Westland DISTILLERY
PEAT WEEK
AMERICAN SINGLE MALT WHISKEY
FIFTH ANNUAL

PEAT WEEK
WESTLAND DISTILLERY
AMERICAN SINGLE MALT
WHISKEY
50% ALC/VOL • (100 PROOF) • 750ML

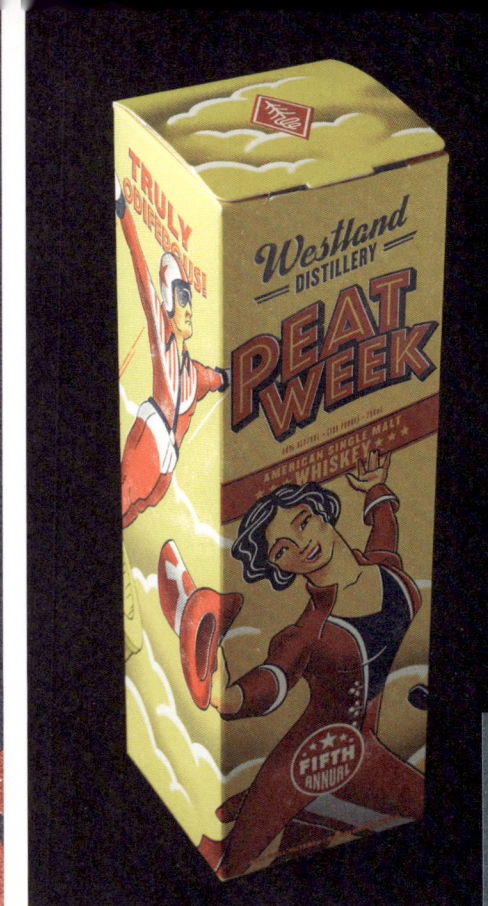

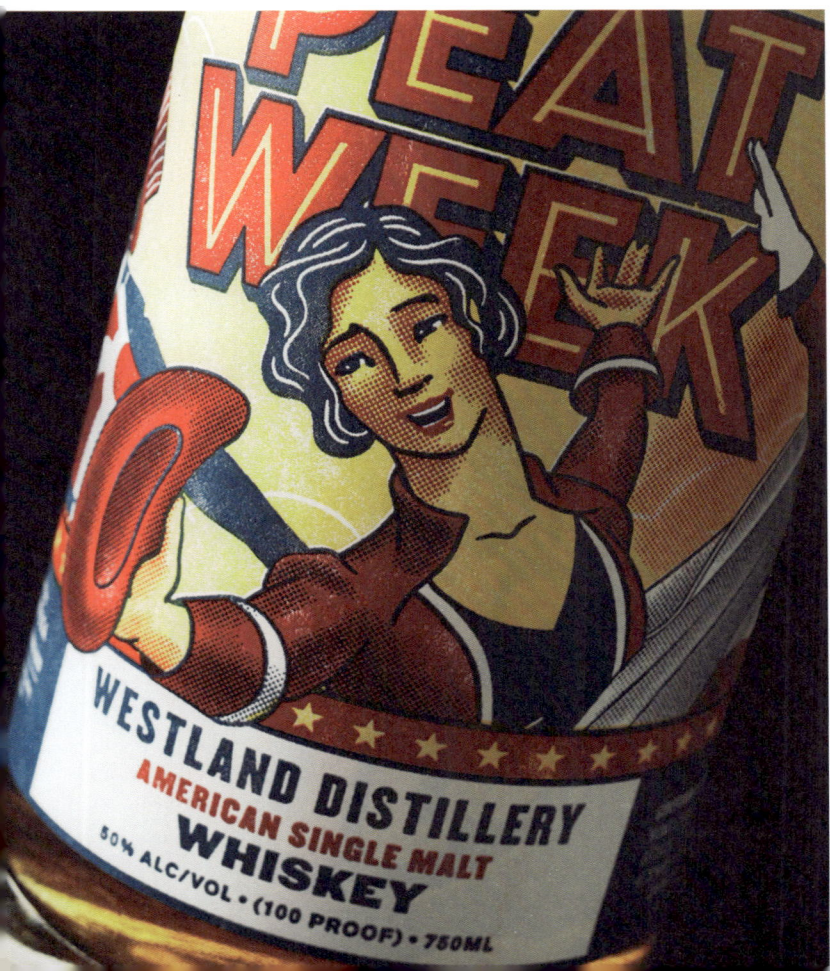

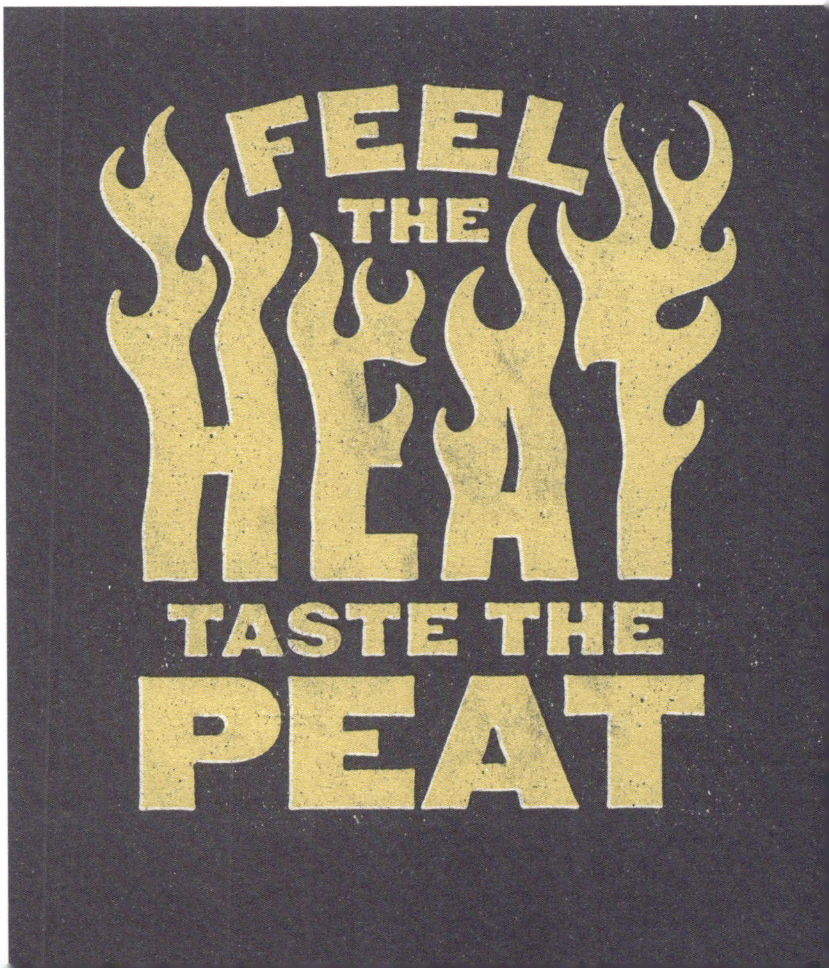
FEEL THE HEAT
TASTE THE PEAT

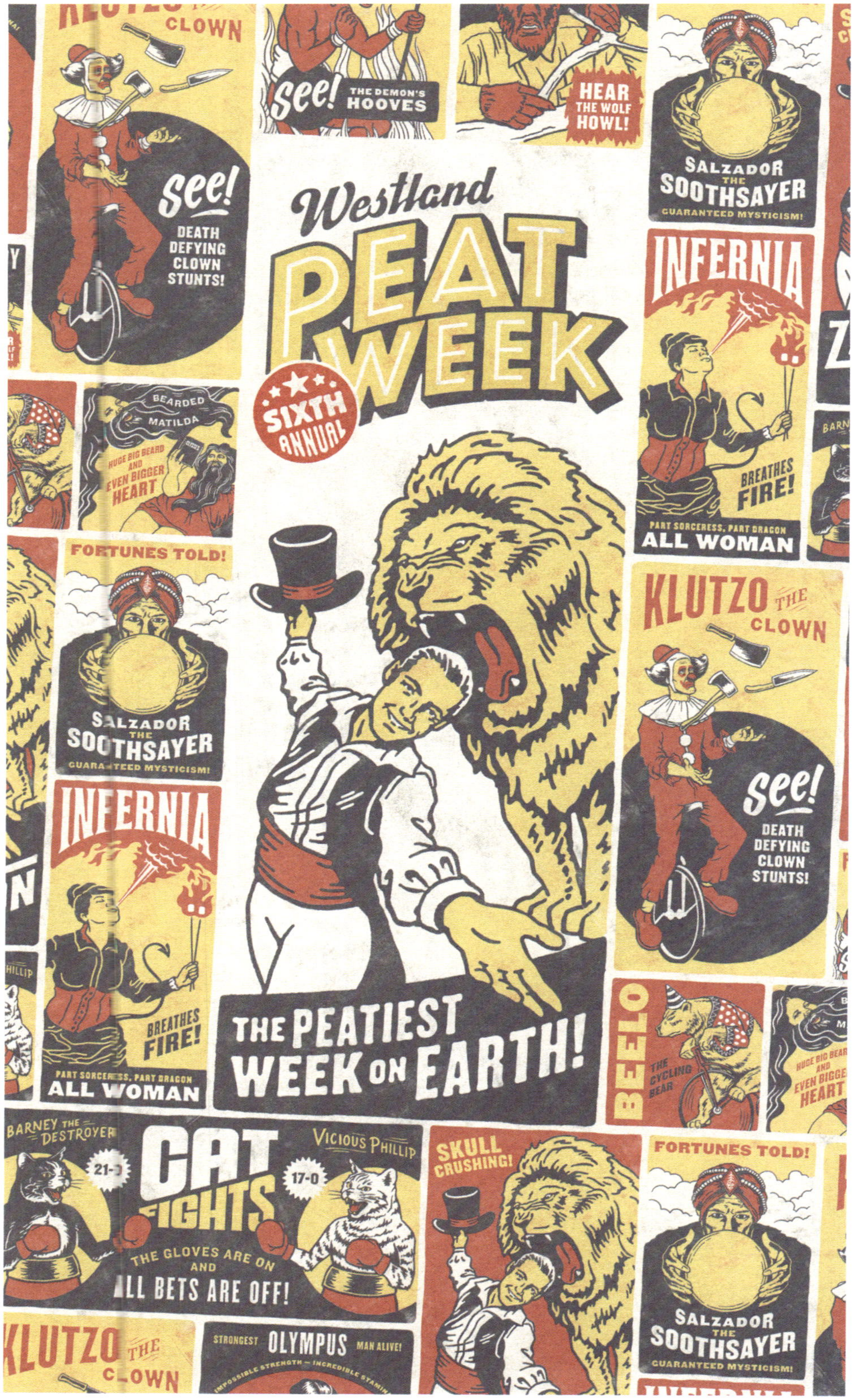

RECONNECTING WHISKEY TO AGRICULTURE

DOUBLE GOLD
TH ANNUAL PEAT WEEK
LD WHISKIES AWARDS
021
GARRYANA EDITION 5
AMERICAN GLE MALT
THE YEAR

WORLD WHISKIES
DISTILLERY MANAG
OF THE Y
BERLIN
INTERNATIONAL SPIRITS COMPETITION 201
USA
PEATED WHISKEY OF THE YEAR

PEATED WESTLAND
AMERICAN SINGLE MALT
WHISKEY
Non Chill Filtered No Coloring Added
Distilled, matured and bottled by
WESTLAND DISTILLERY
SEATTLE, WA U.S.A.
46% ALC/VOL
(92 PROOF)
750ML

WINE ENTHU
TOP 100
SPIRITS IN THE WO
2017
WINT

WORLD WHISKIES AWARDS
2016
WORLD CRAFT PRODUCER
OF THE YEAR

ULTIMATE SPIRITS CHALLENGE 2016
CHAIRMAN'S TROPHY
96 POINTS
AMERICAN
OAK

AMERICAN
DISTILLING 2015 INSTITUTE
WHISKEY OF THE YEAR
PEATED

WORLD W
201
AMERICA
WH
4TH ANNU
NEW YOR

117 | OUR WEST IS WHISKEY

THE WALL OF THE WORLD

by Nate Manny

Our forebears saw the west ahead of them—raw, waiting to be shaped. A place where one could build an idea to match the scale of their surroundings. They were compelled to see the wall of the world as a door to opportunity, its immense rawness a deafening call to work within it.

They laid tracks, crossed ranges, launched ships, rounded capes, and built cities.

Grounded in elemental truths and an ethos of work, their efforts stand today as monuments to the integrity of their principles. Now we must carry forward these ideals and interpret them for our own audacious endeavor.

It was provenance that led us to make single malt whiskey here.

To the north and east, our rolling plains laid with black, fertile soil make the perfect bed for growing barley. Our water, fresh and plentiful, comes as an offering from the snowcapped ridges that surround us. The coastal air, heavy and wise, envelops our casks, just as it does in the glens of the old world. Everything about this place was made ready for this. We had only to hear its call and have the courage to accept its challenge.

Our West is Whiskey—not the untamed frontier of yesteryear. But its challenges are real, its landscape still undeveloped. We are compelled to leverage the nature of ourselves with the unique qualities of the nature that surrounds us to pioneer a new industry for our specific time and place.

And so we head out, with ambition and resolve, to build our future and to shape our West.

We are Westland.

PART FOUR

CULTURAL TERROIR

"I'm a success today because I had a friend who believed in me and I didn't have the heart to let him down."

—

Abraham Lincoln

INSPIRATION & INFLUENCES

by Matt Hofmann

I often speak of whiskey as an extension of culture. While the debate around the impact of environmental terroir, unfortunately, continues to swirl (of course it makes a difference), there is something of a broad consensus on the idea that whiskey is an extension of the place it comes from. Every time you visit a whiskey distillery in Scotland or see brands represented at trade shows, you're undoubtedly going to be swamped with tartan, kilts, and other clichéd symbols of Scottish culture. Or perhaps at times it's a caricature of Scottish culture, something my friends in Ireland call "shamrockery" when they see Irish culture portrayed in the United States.

It's even something I play to, tongue-in-cheek, with our iconic Northwestern flannel shirts I don for these same whiskey events. It's over the top, sure, but it's a way of communicating to whiskey fans that we, and by extension our whiskey, are reflective of the place we call home. This is delivered in a theatrical language that is well understood by people far and wide. Is this genuine? If you're wearing tartan and saying that this represents Scotland, does it mean that everyone in Scotland is like that? Is it about history or the modern day? Some blend of the two?

While we can't speak for the Scotch whisky industry, the idea of Westland being reflective of the culture where it's made was true from the very beginning. Certainly far before we started wearing flannels at trade shows! The really beautiful thing is that Pacific Northwest culture influenced our whiskey before we were really conscious of it and the potential impact it might have. Sure, we set out to make a whiskey from the Pacific Northwest at the beginning, but that process started with a focus on local agriculture and maturation climate. I'd be lying to you if I said we fully grasped the depth and import of cultural impact at our founding.

The thing about living within a culture as you're creating something new is that you don't really notice when it causes you to act a certain way. It doesn't feel like you are "acting" a certain way at all. It just feels natural. It is only when those ways of doing things that feel natural to you bump into expectations about what whiskey "should be" that you begin to realize that you're in fact approaching the subject from a decidedly unique perspective. I began learning about making whiskey in a vacuum. I didn't have any experience or knowledge of Scotch single malt. I wasn't aware of the expectations that were already in place. All I knew was that there was this style of whiskey made from malted barley, a grain that flourishes around the area where I grew up. When you learn this way, you don't have any preconceived notions about what whiskey "should be" in the end. Instead, hungry for knowledge on the subject, you look around to see how other people did it.

While someone starting a distillery in Scotland may see other distilleries around them serve as guideposts, we didn't have any of that tradition here back in 2010. What we did have, however, were breweries. Lots of them. The Pacific Northwest was the epicenter of the craft brewing revolution. It didn't take long for us to see how they looked at malted barley in a completely different way than the whiskey industry did. Brewers (and not just "craft" brewers, mind you) have been utilizing roasted malts for centuries. Roasted malts—malted barley that has been subjected to drying stages with higher temperatures or longer durations, or both—develop new flavor compounds within the grain through a phenomenon called the Maillard reaction. Using the malt's own building blocks of amino acids and sugars, maltsters create a staggering array of aromatics. Dozens of different beer styles, including stouts, porters, amber ales, red ales, and perhaps most poignantly Scotch ales, rely on these hundreds of different types of malts in whole or in part for their unique flavor profile.

Yet in Scotch whisky-making, they used just one—a low-kilned "distiller's malt." I very distinctly remember thinking, "No, that can't be right." The contrast between that and everything I could see in the local brewing

> *"The Pacific Northwest was the epicenter of the craft brewing revolution. It didn't take long for us to see how they looked at malted barley in a completely different way than the whiskey industry did."*

community, from malt supplier websites, homebrew stores, and what little educational literature I could find on whiskey was, frankly, shocking. Honestly, it still is to this day. How did two industries so close to each other, not only geographically but in production processes and raw ingredients, come to view raw ingredients in such a drastically different way?

The influence of the Pacific Northwest and our culture of brewing ultimately won the day at Westland, and the battle wasn't even that close. It just seemed more natural to us, in fact closer to blindingly obvious, that we should be using malted barley as a source of flavor the way that the local brewing industry does. Over time I came to understand that the vast, vast majority of the whiskey industry doesn't even consider malted barley as a source of flavor at all. To most, it is merely as a source of alcohol yield. Despite some evolution from the whiskey industry in the past ten years, I have to say that the brewing industry's approach to malted barley remains much more advanced than that of the world's distillers today, hands down.

This would hold true for another big source of influence to us at Westland, the local wine industry. Washington State is the second biggest winegrowing state in the US outside of California. When we started the distillery, we had two wineries within 100 yards of our front door. A lack of substantive educational material all but forced us to look to this adjacent field for inspiration. There were a few ways that winemakers looked at their subjects that offered something new for us to consider. One in particular stood out right away.

Diving into wine textbooks, you could immediately see that they approached the issue of "oak quality" with more seriousness than what was represented in whiskey texts. Really, the fact that they approached it at all already put them ahead of the whiskey industry. I struggled to find any detail on the subject in the whiskey world, written or otherwise. While the provenance of casks was celebrated, it appeared that the quality of the actual oak wasn't given a second thought. Producers of single malt are quick to champion the idea of flavor coming from the wood, sometimes asserting that 80% of the flavor in a final whiskey comes from the cask. Though we challenge the dogmatic nature of this assertion as a universal

truth, the reality is that there is quite a bit of impact that the wood makes on whiskey, no doubt about it.

However, only in wine textbooks did I see mentions of the ways they would grade the quality of oak lumber that would be suitable for making wine casks. Almost universally, cooperages serving winemakers would use exclusively slow-grown oak, a way of counting the rings per inch of a tree that varies somewhat from cooperage to cooperage. But the gist of it is always the same: the slower the tree grows, the more rings you get per inch. Typically then, the oak becomes more desirable with every additional ring you could fit into that inch of growth.

Winemakers were also intent on air-drying their oak for an extended period of time, usually in excess of 18 months and sometimes up to three years. This has been the traditional methodology used to dry oak staves to the point where they can be utilized for cask construction, but the modern coopering industry has developed a method for shortening that 18 months down to three or four by utilizing a kiln to rapidly dry the wood. The air-drying technique, however, is not used exclusively to remove moisture from the wood. It is still practiced primarily so that the tannins that are naturally present in the oak can be broken down with exposure to the weather, resulting in a softer oak expression in terms of palate astringency and bitterness.

Are there world-class whiskeys made with fast-grown, kiln-dried wood? Yes, of course, because nearly every cask constructed for the whiskey industry is made with this material. Yet winemakers wouldn't touch the stuff. "Kiln dried oak is for furniture," one winemaker once said to me. So why the disconnect?

Why did the brewing industry adopt roasted malts for additional flavor while the single malt industry did not? Why did the wine industry take one perspective on oak while the whiskey industry, globally, took another? The answer, in my opinion, can be summed up in one word: cost. The whiskey industry has been relentlessly focused on reducing costs. To be fair, this business has never boomed quite the way it has today. Sometimes you needed to be frugal to survive. But the fields of brewing and winemaking have had similar ups and downs, and despite the dominance of some low-price macro players in their respective fields, the reverence for quality raw materials still held. Why?

The provocative answer to this question, in my mind, is that whiskey has been a commodity product for the vast majority of its history. So long that it has, in practice, completely forgotten its agricultural roots. Note that I'm not referring to the commodity agricultural system which provides its grains to whiskey (though that has its impacts), but to the commodification of whiskey itself. Whiskey, for the better part of the last 200 years, has been an industrial product for each distillery. Stocks were bought and sold in bulk so that blenders could leverage the differences in flavor profile from each distillery to compose a beautiful whole. Today the whiskey industry can be viewed as the ultimate refined commodity, whereas beer and wine have seen commodification come and go, never quite wiping out their artisanal soul.

The influence of the brewing and winemaking industries on our house style at Westland was not an overt attempt to "create a local influence," it just happened naturally. It was an inherent way of thinking that pointed us down the most obvious, yet at the same time also the most compelling path. These adjacent industries didn't simply change our ideas of what could be added to whiskey, they changed how we even conceive of whiskey itself. I believe, firmly, that if you mention the word "whiskey" to someone who works at Westland, the mental image that is constructed will differ significantly from the one created by someone who works at a distilling "plant" in Scotland. We can't help but see the subject through a different set of lenses, one colored by the brewing industry and the other colored by the winemaking industry.

There are dozens of other influences around us here in the Pacific Northwest, including more from the beer and wine industries. Some are big and obvious, others I'm sure we still haven't even detected yet. Forces measurable in their influence yet perhaps not quite observable in the abstract. At this point in our history, we are aware that local culture is a variable in and of itself that changes the dynamic of the impact of those influences. In other words, we're partially using our own cultural interpretation of the area we call home to shape and guide the variety of ways we come to manifest that culture.

There's something really pure about those first few major influences that came from the wineries and breweries around us, an unintended benefit of starting a distillery thousands of miles away from Scotland. Though we continue to seek out new ways of expanding the idea of what a Pacific Northwest single malt can be, it's always somewhat comforting that we can look back at these influences that revealed themselves in our very first casks of whiskey and know that it still continues on today. A steady sense of continuity. A snapshot of the very first way that we explored Our West and took in the air around us, excited to see something new ahead. With our flannels on, we proudly share this source of Pacific Northwest influence with others around the world.

KINDRED SPIRITS

by Steve Hawley

Too many times now to count, we've run into the dead end of what the traditional whiskey business can give us. The inception of a new idea is thrilling, but in whiskey, it's inevitably followed swiftly by a harsh and dispiriting reality—the established systems in the whiskey industry are incredibly limited and, in fact, inherently designed to erode novel thinking. Were we to confine ourselves solely within the walls of the distillery, reliant only on our keyboards and phones to plug us into that system, the vast majority of our ideas would suffocate in the endless cloud of rebuttals, denials, and outright refusals.

It would be easier to simply accept such limitations and do what we can with what is made available to us. But that is not in our nature. Instead, we head out into the world in search of affirmation. In search of ingenuity. In search of the word "yes."

We've been fortunate to find and befriend some of the brightest minds in fields both related and (previously) unrelated to whiskey. We could argue though that what is equally valuable to their acumen is their courage to stand with us before an obstacle and boldly declare, "We can do that." These are kindred spirits, as consumed by the lure of possibility as we are. We come together to discover answers, build new economies from the ground up, and put shape to new ideas some say are impossible and most say aren't worth the effort.

How we pursue an idea is just as important as the whiskey that ends up in the bottle. Part of that pursuit is a stubborn insistence that there is a better way. Part of it is the shared experiences with those who help us get there. Any whiskey we bottle is a testament to these extraordinary partners, without whom we would have achieved little thus far. We owe them a debt of gratitude and also the solemn promise that our work will never be done.

PHIL NEUMANN
Founder, Mainstem Malting

BRIGID MEINTS
(Fmr) PhD Student, The Bread Lab

RAFA CABELLO
Owner, Tonelería del Sur / Casknolia

DR. STEPHEN JONES
Director, The Bread Lab

STUART WATSON
(Fmr) Director, Forterra

BRANDON SHEARD
Founder, Farmstead Meatsmith

CULTURAL TERROIR | 132

FRANCISCO ROBLES
Owner, Bodegas Robles

TODD DOLLINGER
Founder, ReWine Barrels

CHAD SPALDING
Account Manager, Independent Stave Company

DAVE GREEN
President, Skagit Valley Malting

JOHN ROOZEN
Founder, Washington Bulb Company

KELLY FRIZELL
Master Logger

STEVE LYON
Head Breeder, The Bread Lab

WAYNE CARPENTER
Founder, Skagit Valley Malting

PHIL OLIVERSEN
Operations Manager, Goby Walnut Products

MARK WARD
Founder, Upward Architecture

LOUIE PRAGER
PhD Student, The Bread Lab Barley Fellowship

KENNY WISDOM
Mill Manager, Independent Stave Company

BROTHERS IN BARLEY

by Erik Bennett

The creative spirit of the Pacific Northwest can be hard to encapsulate in any one craft. From the early explorers slowly etching out an economy in the wild to the industries of the present that populate the skylines of our cities, each wave of creative entrepreneurship has evoked supporters and naysayers. But one particular creative endeavor has seemingly united us all, and that is beer. Innovation in American brewing stands in direct contrast to Europe's strict adherence to tradition, and along the way, has provided a framework that has not only allowed for divergent thinking, but encouraged it.

Many of the characters that animated the craft beer revolution began their pursuits in the abandoned buildings and industrial areas of Pacific Northwest cities. They didn't do it because there wasn't any beer to be had. They did it because there was so much more beer to be made. The old world rules that were meant to preserve quality had effectively eliminated flavor and creativity from beer and these brewers were convinced that there was a better way. Like those who had come before, the spirit of the West called and they answered.

Westland was born into this zeitgeist of new thinking, new practices, and new flavors all coming from malted barley. The ethos was almost something to be taken for granted if we weren't careful. Of course malt mattered. But as we quickly realized, the world of single malt whiskey didn't share the same beliefs and we soon found ourselves more closely aligned with our American brothers in barley than our own industry at large. The work done by the early craft brewing community became an inspiration and a reminder to us that just because a practice is expected doesn't mean it should stand eternal.

Through the years, creativity in our local beer scene has continued to expand, even when brewers looked to repurpose time-honored practices such as cask aging beer. Pacific Northwest brewers have been the vanguard of this new world spin on an old world tradition. This fresh wave of experimentation accelerated the need for used casks. Thus, our relationship to the local brewing community turned from inspiration to collaboration and the Westland Cask Exchange program was born.

Cask Exchange, conceived by longtime Westland production team members Scott Sell and Shane Armstrong, looks at the economy of used casks from a new perspective. Instead of the more common practice of selling our casks to the highest bidder, we loan them to kindred spirits in the local brewing scene. We offer no requirement for what type of beer fills these casks, only for them to be returned after use. We know beer finishes are far from novel, but this program isn't about being unique; it's about forging meaningful partnerships and making something together that couldn't have existed before.

To date we have released six bottlings with the Cask Exchange program, but now our rackhouses are filling up with returned and re-filled casks with the potential for some truly special releases in the future. In truth, many of the casks will find their place in whiskeys outside of the Exchange, but the point isn't really the final bottling. Instead, we gain our reward from the trade itself, the giving and receiving of casks but also the camaraderie that comes with it. Cask Exchange is our way of continuing a conversation we've been a part of since our founding—exploring the wonders of this grain that grows so plentifully in our region, with the people who find it just as remarkable as we do.

CASK EXCHANGE RELEASE #1
Release Date: August 2018
Brewing Partner: Kulshan Brewing Co.
Bottle Count: 176

Hailing from the north, this Bellingham-based brewery was an early participant in the Cask Exchange and the first whiskey released. The roasted malts of our house mash bill complemented the chocolate notes of the Imperial Russian Stout previously held by the returned casks. This was the first proof that the whiskeys coming out of this program were of the same caliber as the partnerships behind them.

CASK EXCHANGE RELEASE #2
Release Date: March 2019
Brewing Partner: Black Raven Brewing Co.
Bottle Count: 952

We've worked closely with Black Raven over the years, mostly focused on providing casks for their award-winning beer. So when the opportunity arose to include their exchanged casks in a whiskey release, we were obviously thrilled. The casks selected for blending once held Kriek style and Coffee Stout beers respectively, leading to rich notes of Washington cherries and chocolate.

CASK EXCHANGE RELEASE #3
Release Date: November 2019
Brewing Partner: Silver City Brewery
Bottle Count: 1,130

The Olympic Peninsula is best known for its rocky coast and water-logged rainforest, but like most Pacific Northwest destinations, you have to have a world-class brewery nearby too. Silver City has been brewing on the edge of the wilderness since 1996 and continues to bring that wild spirit to their beers over two decades later. Our whiskey collaboration carried forward this tradition with a pairing of Scotch Ale casks and our 5-malt grain bill that allowed the malty notes of waffle cone to take center stage, complemented by a hint of smoke.

CASK EXCHANGE RELEASE #4
Release Date: June 2020
Brewing Partner: Lucky Envelope Brewing
Bottle Count: 900

Each Cask Exchange release strives to be a thorough collaboration, including the artwork. In this case, we wanted to accurately communicate the tradition of the lucky red envelopes that are the namesake of Lucky Envelope Brewing, located in the burgeoning brewery scene in the Ballard neighborhood of Seattle. The resulting label captures the energy of celebration and makes this whiskey the perfect dram for any special occasion.

CASK EXCHANGE RELEASE #5
Release Date: December 2020
Brewing Partner: Holy Mountain Brewing Co.
Bottle Count: 1,065

Although there are many more Cask Exchange whiskeys to come, our release with Holy Mountain has left a distinct mark on the series. Channeling the heavy metal vibes of our partners in cask, this whiskey pulls no punches by elevating the Port casks, American Strong Beer, and malt-forward mash bill to an equal fever pitch where you lose nothing and gain everything. A memorable partnership to be sure, perhaps it won't be the last.

CASK EXCHANGE RELEASE #6
Release Date: August 2021
Brewing Partner: Bellwether Brewing Co.
Bottle Count: 500

When we exchange casks, we make sure there are no strings attached, allowing the brewer to take full creative license. Bellwether Brewing Co. from Spokane in Eastern Washington took us at our word, and returned the casks after using them to age a variety of Belgian style beers along with a unique pine resin addition. This release widens the series in both geography and variety of flavors introduced in the Exchange.

CULTURAL TERROIR | 140

ALL KIDDING ASIDE

by Steve Hawley

There's no denying that single malt whiskey has an image problem. The stuffy, old curmudgeon pontificating from a tufted red leather wingback chair is still the prevailing persona, and it's not entirely untrue. The whiskey industry is trying—to be more inclusive, more contemporary, more interesting—but sometimes we just can't get out of our own way. It's confounding how we often perpetuate, consciously or not, the stereotypes. Westland is no exception. We take our work seriously. We can be bookish, to put it mildly, and that can be intimidating or even alienating to many.

Thankfully, a resplendent American holiday can save us from our pretentions. Since 2015, Westland has celebrated April Fool's Day with a limited release of single malt aimed squarely at the funny bone. This new tradition helps us take ourselves a little less seriously and reminds our team and our fans that whiskey should be fun after all. Of course, as is our way, April Fool's Day isn't purely about the hijinks. It's also an opportunity for commentary on the tired tropes of the whiskey business.

Each year we take the opportunity to poke fun at some of the more preposterous or nonsensical trends and customs in single malt whiskey that tend to keep it mired in its stodgy ways. We've parodied the preciousness of cask finishing with Inferno, lamented predictable and shallow tasting notes with Boldsmooth, raised an eyebrow about "lifestyle" whiskeys with Sport Dram, lampooned the trend of celebrity whiskeys with Celebrious, and collectively rolled our eyes at whiskey procured solely for the purpose of investment with The Inheritance. In the end, the satire is all in good humor and made at no one's expense. For Westland, April Fool's Day offers us the chance to shake the establishment a bit, be outspoken in a new way, and demonstrate that there's room in single malt whiskey for more than cigars and cravats (not that there's anything wrong with either of those wonderful things).

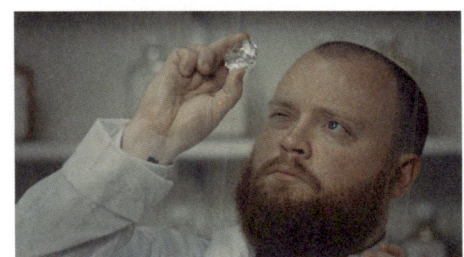

CULTURAL TERROIR | 144

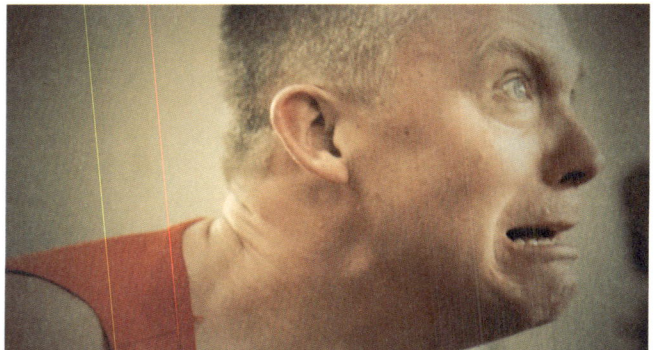

Winning is for the strong.
That's why you train.
Because muscles are for winning.
And winners are born thirsty.
Sport Dram is for the strong.
The brutal.
The thirsty.
Sport Dram is for the winners.
KLENCH THE KWENCH!

In the age of celebrities, and the spirits that celebrate them. In a world where everyone can have their moment in the spotlight, there is a new star rising...

Any celebrity worth 15 minutes of fame deserves their own whiskey.

A whiskey that says, "I've made it!"

Now you can count yourself among the echelon of the elite. You are one of the rare few to have the adoration of thousands, and the whiskey to prove it.

This is your moment, this is your whiskey.

CELEBRIOUS!

CULTURAL TERROIR | 146

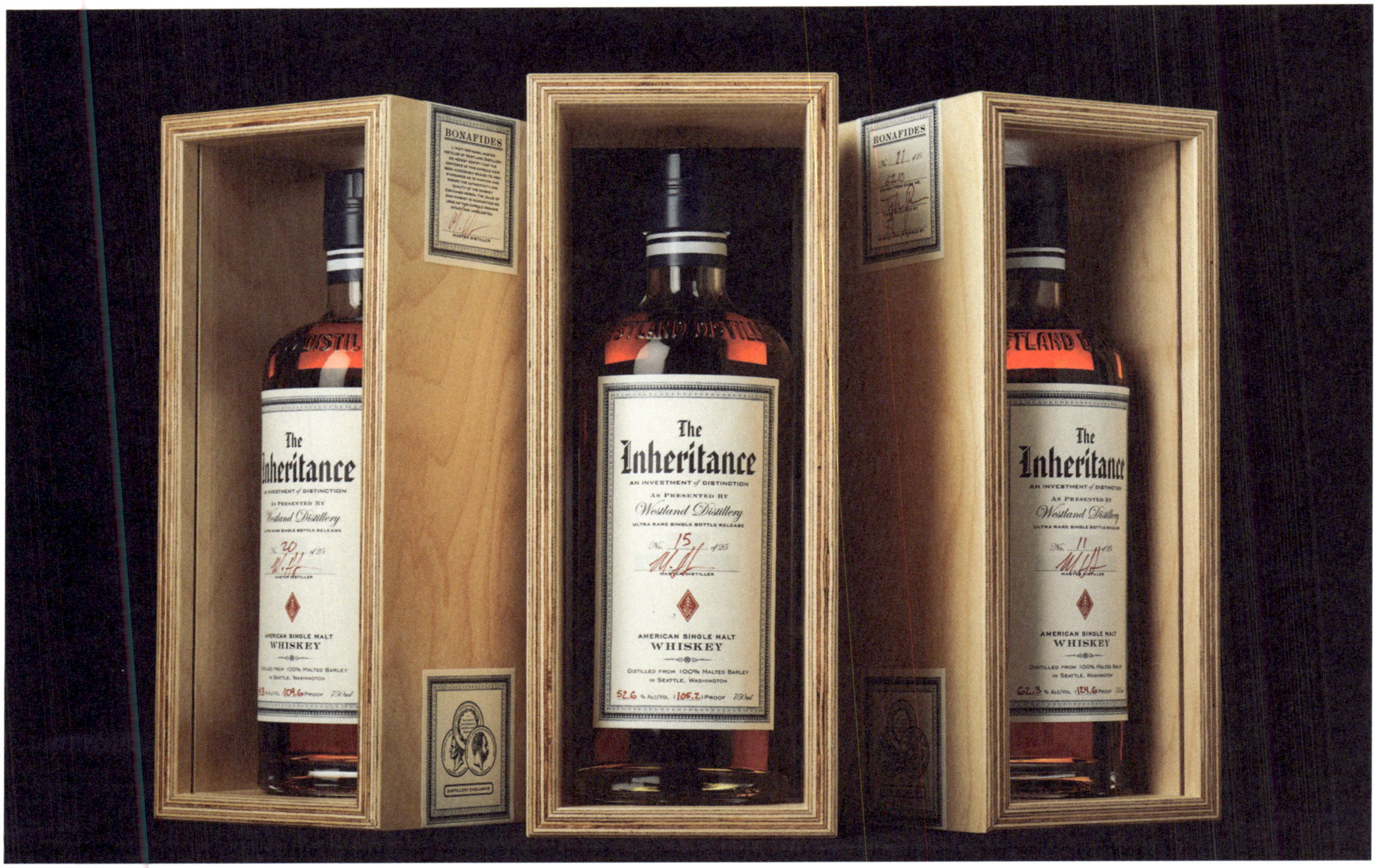
BONAFIDES
The Inheritance
AN INVESTMENT of DISTINCTION
AS PRESENTED BY
Westland Distillery
ULTRA RARE SINGLE BOTTLE RELEASE
No. 15 of 25
AMERICAN SINGLE MALT
WHISKEY
DISTILLED FROM 100% MALTED BARLEY
IN SEATTLE, WASHINGTON

The Inheritance
AN INVESTMENT of DISTINCTION
AS PRESENTED BY
Westland Distillery
RARE SINGLE BOTTLE WHISKEYS
AUCTION CATALOG
04|01|21
AMERICAN SINGLE MALT
WHISKEY
Inheritance
AN INVESTMENT of DISTINCTION
AS PRESENTED BY
Westland Distillery
No. 15 of 25
ULTRA-RARE SINGLE BOTTLE RELEASE
DISTILLERY EXCLUSIVE
HH-EXB / MADEIRA
CASK TYPE
S. SELL

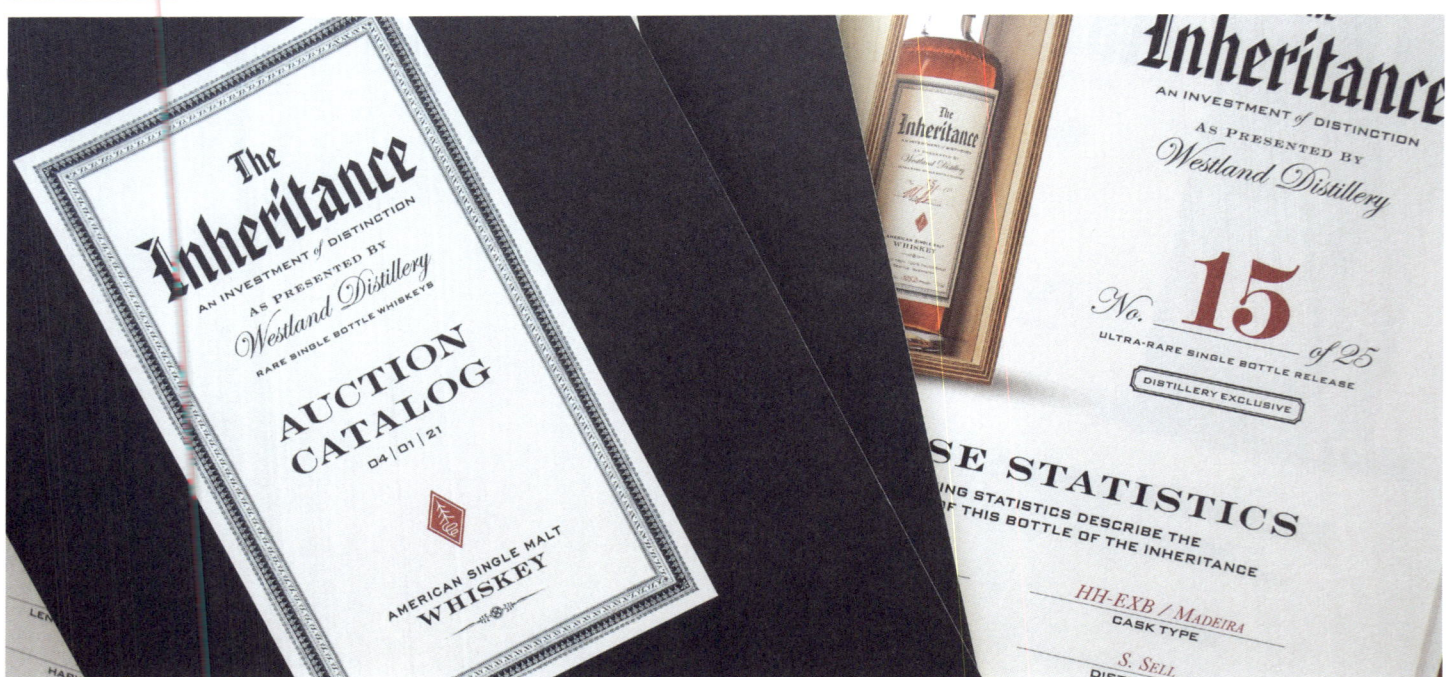

NEW ROADS THROUGH ANDALUCÍA

by Steve Hawley

As producers of single malt whiskey in America, we face an interesting dilemma: How do we balance tradition, authenticity, innovation, quality, and truth? How do we respect the foundation that was laid before us but contribute something new as well? The majority of our industry trades on a history that was written a long time ago. But despite the polished veneer of consistency that the malt whiskey industry paints itself with, the reality is nothing in this business has ever been static. While it's easy to be swept up in the conventional and very successful narrative of tradition, we must be honest with ourselves when the current plot being written by Scotland doesn't work for us.

At Westland, we endeavor to make the most authentic single malt whiskey we can in the Pacific Northwest. This means we are embracing the raw materials and culture of our region. At the same time we also must balance this against aspects of tradition that still hold meaning—notions that are especially predominant in our business. We have no intention of throwing out the proverbial baby with the bathwater. In this industry, there is a long list of traditions that we respect and uphold. There are many examples of traditional whiskey-making practiced at Westland—some obvious, many more subtle. One of the most obvious traditions we've carried forward is the use of Sherry wine casks in maturation.

But with many aspects of tradition there is an interpretation that must take place—an interpretation commanded by the passing of time.

Pretending what once was will always be is foolhardy. We can't be afraid to question conventions to ensure they are relevant to the ideals we espouse in our own time and place. At Westland, we work hard not to simply rent the narrative from Scotland. Instead, we find in its traditions what can be true to us and true now. For Westland, what is compelling about Sherry wine casks is the historical relationship of a wine region to the whiskey business, not necessarily about the flavor of the casks specifically. Creating our own relationship is how we can fit into the ongoing tradition. That pursuit begins in Andalucía, the home of Sherry wines.

Before we can begin to describe what our relationship with Andalusian wines might look like, we must try to understand what the landscape of the region offers, both figuratively and quite literally. "Sherry" is frequently misunderstood, especially in the United States. Not only is it a style of wine, but a wine region in and of itself. In fact, the "Sherry" Denominación de Origen (D.O.) was the first of its kind in Spain. This region is formed by a triangular area, with three cities as the vertices: Jerez, El Puerto de Santa María, and Sanlúcar de Barrameda. A coastal area in southwestern Spain, the famous Sherry Triangle makes a style of wine informed by both the realities of its climate and soils, as well as the ports from which the wine was and is shipped. The moderating effect of the Atlantic Ocean, bringing in higher humidity and reducing daytime high temperatures, creates a few dynamics.

First, the high humidity of the Sherry Triangle favors growth of one particular varietal of wine grape, Palomino, over another, Pedro Ximénez. Pedro Ximénez grapes have difficulty with high humidity environments and thus their use is usually restricted to the drier climates of inland Andalucía. While many of the wines from further inland reach incredible levels of alcohol that render them biologically stable for transportation, the Sherry Triangle typically utilizes additions of neutral spirit for fortification to achieve the same stability.

Because Palomino grapes have less potential for high sugar yield relative to Pedro Ximénez, they almost always naturally ferment to dryness. What to do if you would like to add some sweetness to the wine? Enter "PX" wine. In one of the ironic twists of the Sherry D.O., there is one exception to the rule that all Sherry wines must be produced in the Sherry Triangle. In order to achieve some sweetness, PX wine from the Montilla-Moriles region is legally permitted to be imported and blended. PX is a style of wine made from the high sugar yield of the Pedro Ximénez grape and a process of sun-drying them to substantially increase the concentration the of these sugars. Thus, many of the most famous styles of Sherry wine such as "Cream Sherry" (an Oloroso wine blended with a PX wine for sweetness) and PX wine itself, source not just the grapes but the actual wine from outside of the Sherry region, either in part or even in full.

So, what does it mean to make a Sherry cask-matured whiskey that is still authentic to us in the Pacific Northwest? How do you choose the right balance between history, tradition, innovation, quality, and reality? Certainly the answer to that question is subjective. But we believe the interpretation of this perfect balancing act is what defines a distillery's Sherry cask program, rather than the taste.

We always view our lack of single malt whiskey-producing history as a double-edged sword. It's an opportunity to explore new roads in a long-standing industry that places a tremendous value on history. But, fundamentally, that history is not ours. It would be both disingenuous and less interesting to try to claim it was. We must find our own way of relating to the traditions of whiskey within the context of our own perspective and ambitions.

Like much of whiskey production historically, the use of Sherry wine casks was driven by economic realities. The popularity of Sherry wine in the UK during the 19th century flooded the market with wine casks used for transportation, back when a cask was considered solely a container for storage and shipping rather than an "ingredient." Though Sherry wine slowly transitioned away from shipping in casks by the early 20th century, another cultural force provided a new source. Oddly enough, it was the exact opposite of the paradigm that led to the custom in the first place. People stopped drinking Sherry.

"We must find our own way of relating to the traditions of whiskey within the context of our own perspective and ambitions."

As wineries started to close in Spain, more and more casks became available to whiskey producers in Scotland. Unlike most other wine styles, Sherry producers keep and use their casks for decades or longer. So while the tradition of using Sherry wine casks for whiskey maturation continued, the historical mechanism for feeding that tradition began to break down. As the appetite for Sherry cask-matured whiskey grew, the demand for Sherry casks began to far exceed the demand for the wine maturing within them. Speaking with an acclaimed producer of Sherry in Jerez, we learned that, to counter that change, producers have devised several methods for getting the casks that they want, or more specifically, the flavor they want.

In the 1970s and 80s, the primary solution to this problem was Paxarette, a more obscure style of wine made with Pedro Ximénez grapes, some of which have been concentrated. Paxarette, however, wasn't being matured in casks. Instead, it was poured—500ml to 1,000ml of wine typically—

into a cask, pressurized inside until the Paxarette was absorbed into the wood, then discarded. To us, this is crossing a line. It's a subtle line, but one that we think is really important. In using wine to exclusively flavor the wood, with no regard for its quality as a wine, truth was lost. It was replaced by a shallow attempt to chase a flavor profile without investing in the culture, authenticity, and industry of the region.

Today, a similar model is quietly used by a number of Sherry producers and their malt whiskey clients. A low grade of Sherry is being manufactured, again specifically designed to flavor the cask, before then being used for bulk ethanol distillation or vinegar production, if not discarded. This grade of Sherry is designated only for cask flavoring and not suitable for bottling using the Sherry Wine D.O. Like the use of Paxarette, there's something inherently inauthentic about this practice, at least to us. If the Sherry used to flavor

the cask cannot legally be called Sherry wine afterwards—even if it tastes similar to the real thing—is that staying true to the history of the practice? This is the question that each whiskey producer will have to ask themselves. For most, the use of Sherry casks is about the continuation of a flavor profile, even if the route to get there is different from the past. There's a huge incentive to keep that practice going too. There is a familiarity with the flavor profile that many brands have built their following on. There is certainly global demand for it. Perhaps though, if there were more of a focus on the other ingredients, especially barley, by malt whiskey producers it wouldn't be so dire an issue.

At Westland, we view our Sherry cask program through a different lens. While the realities of the trade have changed over time, we believe the fundamental spirit of the tradition should remain. At the core of this long tradition it is less about a flavor. It is more about the relationship our business and industry has to the region of Andalucía and its wine industry.

"Andalucía is soaked in wine and culture. The nuances of both are important to understand and embrace."

Andalucía is soaked in wine and culture. The nuances of both are important to understand and embrace. On our visits to Spain, to meet and work with our partners there, it is the culture of the place that always leaves the greatest impression. It guides our vision for our whiskey and reminds us that the evolving tradition isn't a means to an end, but a compelling part of what makes whiskey a rewarding pursuit.

In her fabulous book, *Sherry: A Modern Guide to the Wine World's Best Kept Secret*, Talia Baiocchi offers a piece of advice to visitors: "Never, ever come to this part of Spain and show up to a meeting on time. You will startle and confuse your host." We learned this firsthand on our early visits, even if it took some time to get used to. It's charming for sure, but also poignant. As you settle into the way of Andalucía and its wines, it is these small aspects of the culture that underscore the importance of treating the wines and the process with reverence. This is where we can connect to the people we work with, forming relationships based on a shared belief that every component of the process is important—that each ingredient and each person along the way is valued.

Every Sherry cask that we fill at Westland was used to produce high-quality, authentic Sherry wine. The casks we've received to date are mostly from wineries that have decreased production or gone out of business, something we know is not sustainable in the long term. Either the wineries will all go out of business, in which case there will be no authentic Sherry left. Or, hopefully, the fortunes of the Sherry wine business will continue its revival. We believe strongly that it is our responsibility as a whiskey producer utilizing Sherry wine casks to do our part in supporting that revival even if it presents us with a new problem. If the Sherry industry does indeed rebound, they won't have a reason to sell their casks anymore.

Like the rest of the world, Andalucía is changing. We must change with it. Driving the streets of Jerez, we often find our way to new, smaller bodegas tucked alongside larger, familiar signs and buildings that seem more like museums and facades than growing concerns. These new bodegas, speckled amongst the relics of a once-celebrated past, those that are set in their ways (or at least used to be when there were ways), are bringing renewed vitality and creativity to an industry that must evolve to survive. We find the same thing outside the Sherry Triangle where we're working with bodegas that have developed inventive techniques for seasoning new casks and delivering unique flavor profiles without ever once considering compromising the wine we're left with in the end. Technically, casks from these regions outside the Sherry Triangle wouldn't even be considered "Sherry" casks but that doesn't make them any less interesting. There is a world to be explored if we open our minds to new possibilities.

We all have a choice to make in how we participate in the evolving tradition of Sherry cask-matured whiskey. Do we honor the culture of the region and contribute to its renaissance? Or do we try to recreate the past with imitations that don't respect the wine itself in the hopes that we can continue to simply outpace the trend at the expense of Andalucía's economy and people? That's an easy choice for us at Westland. We relish the opportunity to form our own relationship with this remarkable region and play even a small part in the next chapter of the Andalusian wine industry.

SUSTAINABILITY IN WHISKEY

by Steve Hawley

Sustainability in whiskey is a complicated matter, certainly more so today than it was a decade ago. It can be elusive, while at the same time becoming more pressing as each day passes. In many ways, sustainability is easy to prioritize in words, but harder to realize in action. Of us it requires both broad, holistic planning and smaller, more immediate choices in our daily work.

For a distillery that touts its connection to the land and champions its whiskey as a reflection of provenance, it's imperative that we be good stewards of that place. We do so in process, in sourcing, and in a commitment to restoration. Be that water-saving equipment, investments in ecologically friendly barley breeding, designing new methods for harvesting and processing peat, or simply rolling up our sleeves and planting 600 oak tree saplings, we seek to do our part in repaying the region that gives us so much.

We're lucky in that we can do more as a company than most individuals are able to alone and we embrace that responsibility with reverence. But we also recognize that this is a long-play game where progress is measured in incremental, and sometimes imperceptible steps. As whiskey-makers we're practiced at the art of patience. We only need to remind ourselves that, like whiskey, stewardship is a mindset, not an endgame.

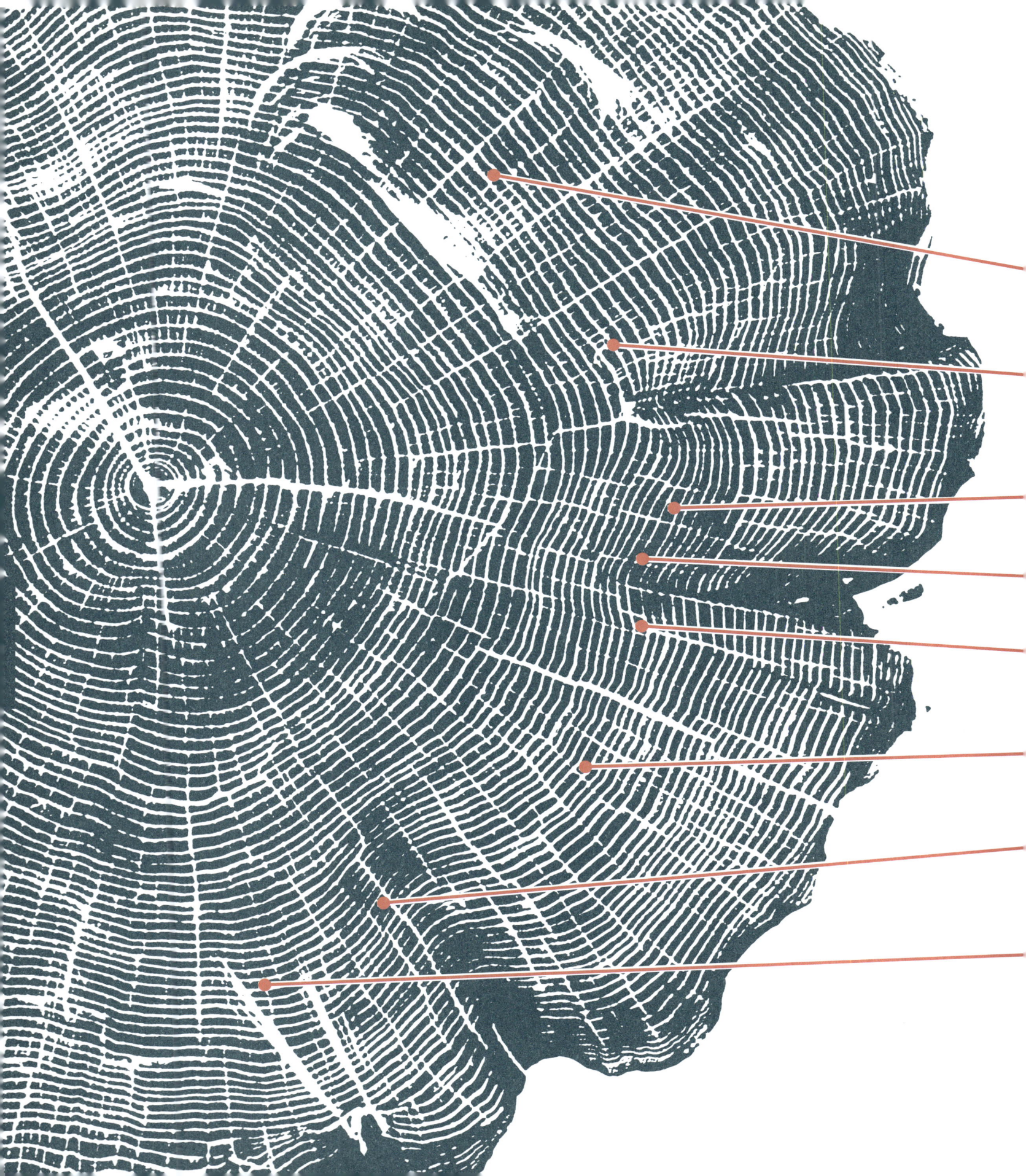

THE PROGRESS OF WESTLAND 2016–2017

A POINT OF VIEW

With each passing day we deepened our connection to Pacific Northwest provenance and with it, our conviction that whiskey with a sense of place was supremely worthwhile. In these years we became ever more outspoken about those beliefs. Westland had something to say, something new and uniquely American, and we were going to say it.

1 JANUARY 2016: FIRST WASHINGTON STATE PEAT DISTILLATION
Up until this time, there was no peated malt from America available, let alone from our home state. So we built the supply chain, from the ground down.

2 MARCH 2016: WHISKY MAGAZINE WORLD CRAFT PRODUCER OF THE YEAR
While we've had a long and complicated relationship with the word "craft," we were honored to be recognized with this award by one of the most prestigious competitions in the world. It was not only validation for Westland, but for American Single Malt as a category.

3 MARCH 2016: ASMW COMMISSION FOUNDING
In the midst of a blizzard on Chicago's north side, Westland assembled a small group of distillers from across the country to define American Single Malt Whiskey and form the trade body to establish, promote, and protect the category across the world.

4 APRIL 2016: ULTIMATE SPIRITS CHALLENGE CHAIRMAN'S TROPHY
Further evidence that Westland single malt could stand with the finest whiskeys in the world.

5 JUNE 2016: GARRYANA EDITION 1 RELEASE
In what would become Westland's most critically acclaimed and highly anticipated annual limited release, Garryana represents the pinnacle of exploration in single malt.

6 NOVEMBER 2016: WINTER RELEASE
Outside of the Core Range and what would become the Outpost Range, Winter sealed Westland's reputation for inventive and delicious bespoke bottlings.

7 JANUARY 2017: WESTLAND JOINS RÉMY COINTREAU
To realize our potential, Westland needed a partner with a global reach that could help us build for the next phase and beyond. In Rémy Cointreau we gained a partner that shares our passion for brands rooted in terroir and our vision for building generational businesses.

8 FEBRUARY 2017: GARRY OAK RESTORATION
While this is a commitment that will long outlast anyone currently at Westland, you must begin somewhere. On this date, we planted our first in what would become hundreds of Garry Oak saplings in Washington State, restoring critical habitat that had been lost.

CULTURAL TERROIR

CULTURAL TERROIR | 168

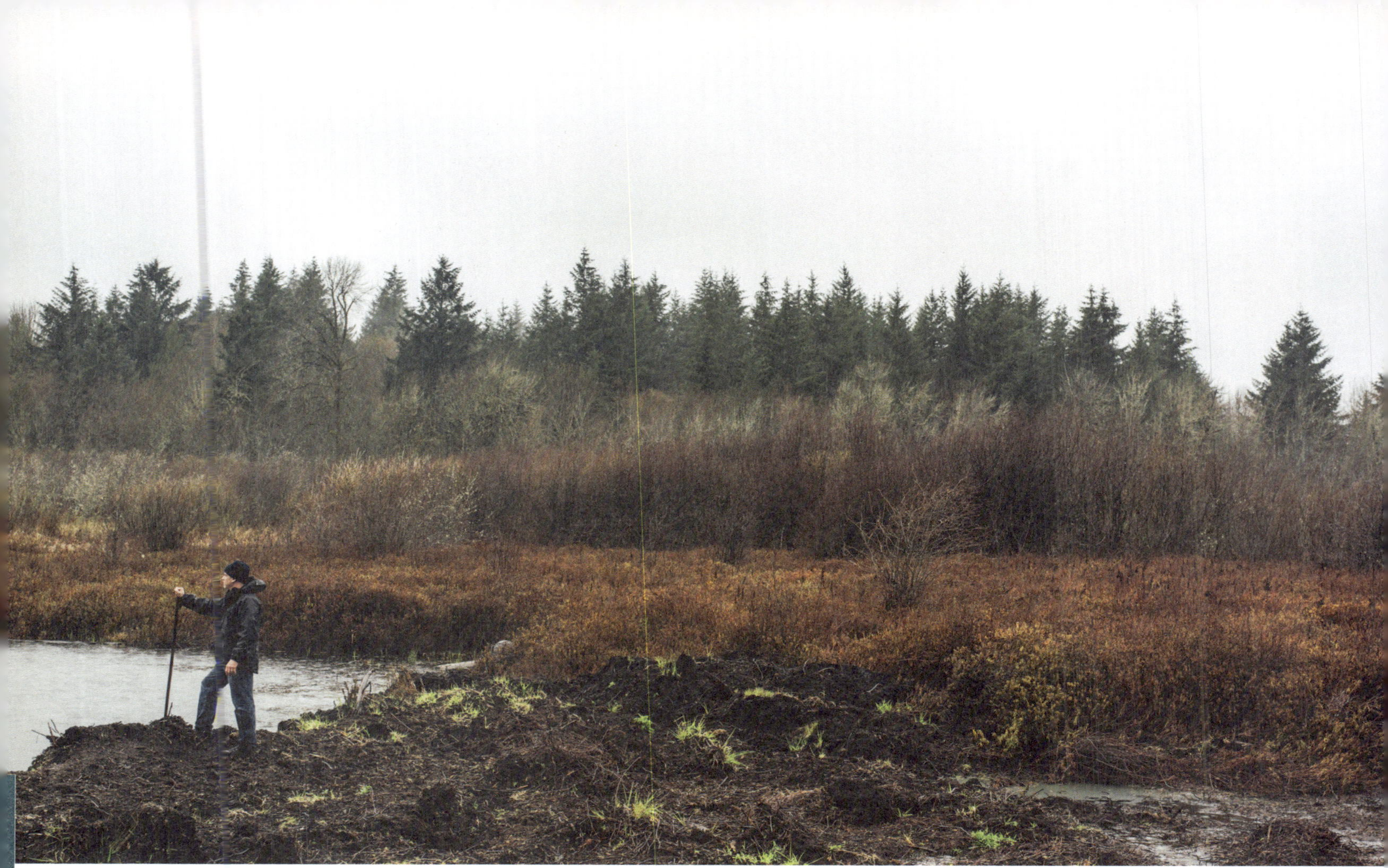

SHERRY WOOD
WESTLAND
AMERICAN SINGLE MALT
WHISKEY
Non Chill Filtered
No Coloring Added
Distilled, matured and bottled by
WESTLAND DISTILLERY
SEATTLE, WA U.S.A.
46% ALC/VOL
(92 PROOF)
750ML

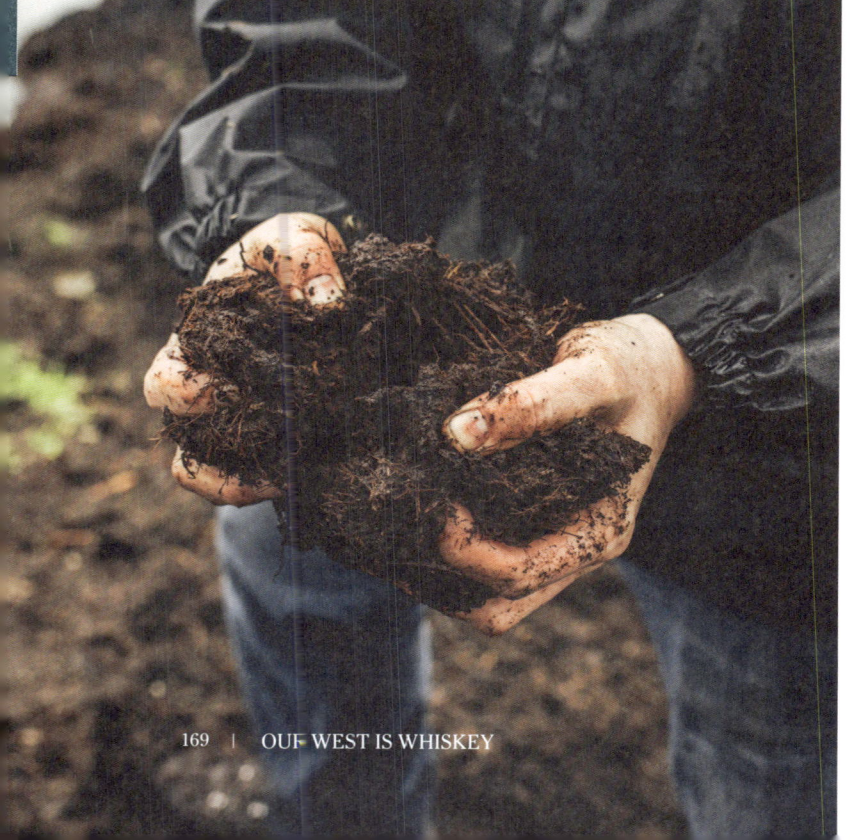

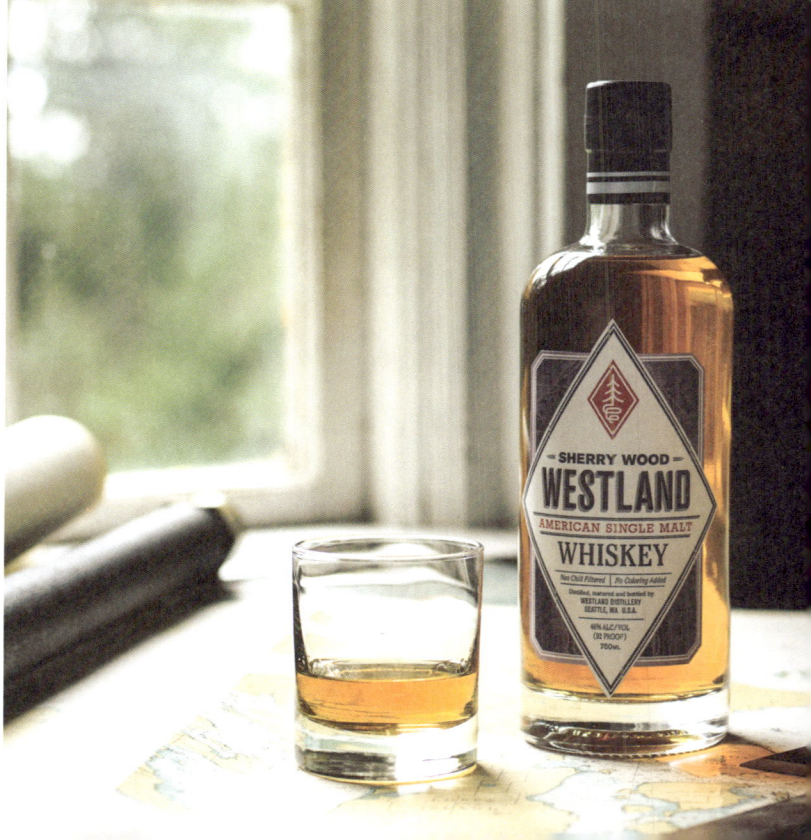

CULTURAL TERROIR | 170

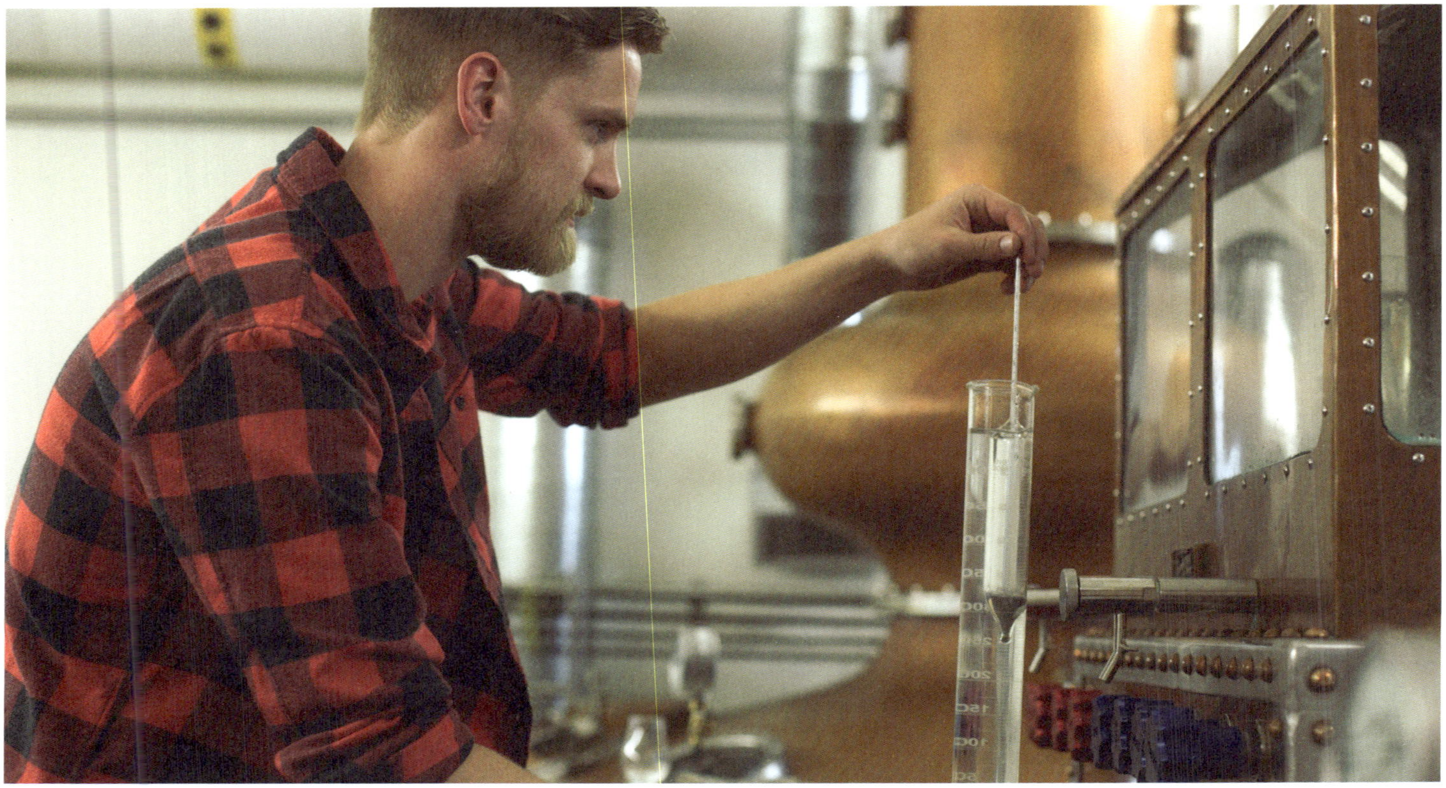

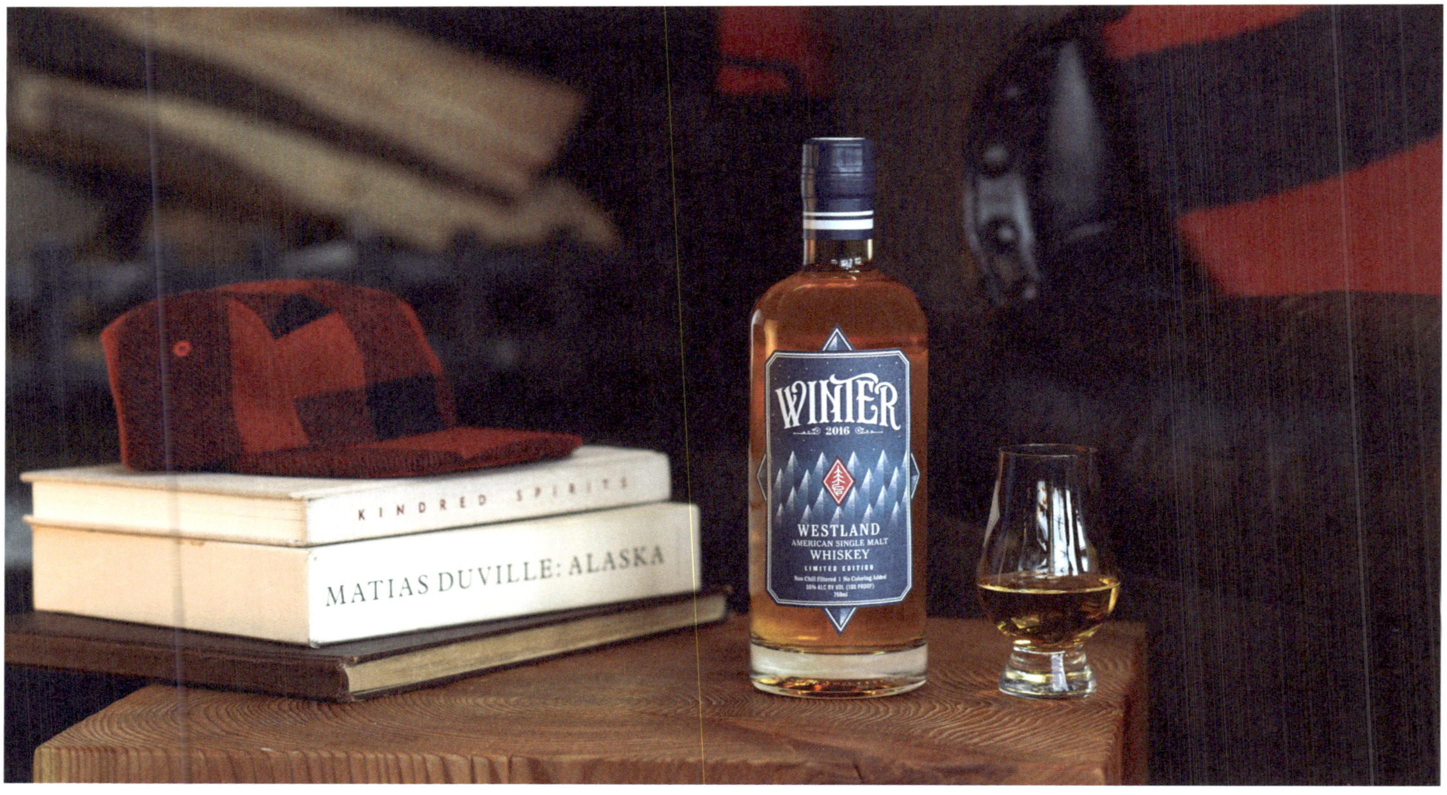
WINTER
2016
WESTLAND
AMERICAN SINGLE MALT
WHISKEY
LIMITED EDITION
KINDRED SPIRITS
MATIAS DUVILLE: ALASKA

CULTURAL TERROIR | 172

PART FIVE

WHISKEY FOR A NEW WORLD

"You can't depend on your eyes when your imagination is out of focus."

—

Mark Twain

UNVEILING WHISKEY

by Becky Paskin

London-based blender Compass Box was long known for its unconventional publication of full, detailed recipes for its blends, including the whisky's origin, the cask types used, and their proportions in the final product.

But in 2015 it went one step further, releasing the ages of each component whisky in two new blends: This Is Not A Luxury Whisky and Flaming Heart. In doing so, it crossed a line. Both expressions were found to have broken Scotch whisky regulations and EU law, which state that distillers can only disclose the youngest component of any spirit.

This was a blow for Compass Box founder John Glaser, an advocate for full transparency in Scotch whisky, who, with the support of several other producers, unsuccessfully attempted to have the law amended.

Although the regulation was originally designed to prevent producers from over-emphasising the role of older whiskies in a blend, Glaser claimed the proposed amendment would have given consumers "greater clarity around what it is they're buying and… help the Scotch industry stay relevant in a world where provenance and transparency are increasingly relevant."

He was certainly onto something. Consumers are more concerned than ever about the origins of their food and drink. From meat and dairy to coffee and chocolate, they want assurances that the products they're purchasing are ethically made and sourced, have a negligible carbon footprint, and contain no surprising hidden ingredients. They also have a natural curiosity surrounding how flavours are created, prompting interest in production processes and raw materials. In fact, recent research from Innova Marketing Insights shows almost two-thirds of global consumers are now interested in learning where their food comes from.

Much of this demand is being driven by the "era of distrust"—fake news, data breaches, and privacy concerns have heightened our scepticism. As a result, 86% of Americans believe transparency is now more important than ever according to Sprout Social.

Glaser's legal challenge may have failed, but the controversial incident was a pivotal moment in the ongoing conversation around transparency in whisky. Today, the topic has expanded beyond age to encompass provenance, terroir, processes, sustainability, and company ethics—a whole spectrum of issues that consumers regard as important. It's filtered into the philosophies of maverick whisky makers around the world who share the same values of authenticity and openness.

Not too long ago the whisky industry was a surreptitious environment. Recipes were closely safeguarded secrets, processes hidden behind closed doors, distillers forbidden from speaking to one another. Over time, and with the rise of world whisky and curious consumers, producers have realised the merits of sharing experiences and information. They've realised that a rising tide raises all ships and how the advancement of distilleries around the world can benefit the whole category.

Transparency has since become a buzz word of the modern global whisky industry, but it comes with both positive and negative implications.

The most powerful advantage of greater transparency is that it generates trust, building a stronger relationship between brands and consumers who appreciate openness and honesty. They feel part of the conversation and brought into the brand's narrative.

Clarity over provenance, terroir, and production processes can connect consumers with distilleries and their "spirit of place." With the rise of world whisky this connection has never been more important. Many distillers are speaking more loudly about their farmer partners, the local maltsters processing their grains, and even nearby breweries and wineries involved in cask exchange programmes. In doing so they are building not only a local community, but a global following as well.

Some whisky producers have even adopted blockchain technology (the tech used to track cryptocurrency) to ensure every process and movement in their whisky's journey is logged and traced from field to bottle. This not only draws the consumer into the brand story, heightening their appreciation of the product, but proves authenticity and provenance while remaining fully transparent.

When most whisky consumers think of transparency, they likely imagine full disclosure of the production process, cask makeup, ages, and source of whisky in the bottle. Full transparency of a whisky's recipe is a refreshing and still novel occurrence, but it can provide drinkers with a greater understanding of how flavour is created.

For instance, a rye whisky made with 60% rye, 30% wheat and 10% malted barley will be softer and more floral than a spicy, full-bodied 100% rye whiskey. A single malt made from chocolate malt and matured in first-fill ex-Sherry casks will be a bigger, bolder, and sweeter whisky than a pale malt matured in refill hogsheads. This information can simultaneously improve consumers' knowledge and help them navigate the whisky category, provided they already understand how each component translates into flavour.

Full transparency about intricate production processes, such as fermentation times, wash strength, and cut points can be useful information for whisky lovers wanting to learn more about their favourite whiskies. However, they can be confusing and off-putting for newcomers if those facts are not accompanied by the why. Why does a long fermentation matter? What does a low wash strength mean? Why use chocolate malt or pilsner? What impact do these ingredients or processes have on the whisky in my glass? Transparency works only when the consumer understands what the producer is being transparent about.

"Full transparency of a whisky's recipe is a refreshing and still novel occurrence, but it can provide drinkers with a greater understanding of how flavour is created."

While a lot of coverage about transparency in whisky is focused on the product itself, really the ideal stretches deeper into the root of company culture and how brands communicate with their audiences.

Today's consumer wants to hear from the people behind the brand, the distillers and blenders, the ambassadors and brand owners. In the spirit of transparency, company spokespeople should be allowed to speak from the heart and in their own voice. Too often they're not trusted to speak candidly, with company policy dictating they regurgitate a robotic script.

In a refreshing twist, some start-up distillers are taking a more sincere, personal approach by admitting to the successes and failures of their early days, holding their hands up to mistakes, and crediting others who've helped them along the way. They're retelling the true stories of how partnerships were formed (plot twist: it almost always happens over a glass of whisky), and openly talk about the experiments that just didn't work.

Real transparency is about admitting to flaws, making information accessible, and cultivating a culture of honesty. This approach has its rewards—85% of consumers will stay loyal to brands through a crisis if they have a track record of transparency according to Sprout Social. It boils down to trust, and no amount of openness about a whisky's cask breakdown will make up for perceived secrecy in other areas.

"Real transparency is about admitting to flaws, making information accessible, and cultivating a culture of honesty."

It's more than just honesty, it's choosing to lay bare every aspect of a whisky's story, from its owner's philosophies and ethical conduct to production process and ingredients. Some whisky companies have been lauded for their candidness, but how transparent is transparent enough, and how much do we as consumers need to know about a whisky in order to just enjoy it?

Are consumers satisfied just to know part of the story, like where and how their whisky has been produced, or will they evolve to demand full recipes a la Compass Box, which may infringe on producers' intellectual property? Why should the world's biggest-selling brands risk imitation by divulging the exact recipe for their blends, simply because consumers demand it of them? The truth is, these massive brands that sell millions of litres of whisky each year are made to taste rather than specific measurements, so any recipe would be out of date the moment it's published.

Six years after the publication of Compass Box's controversial recipes, and with transparency a trending topic, where does that leave Glaser's war on Scotch age statements? Luckily, he and a supportive band of other distillers found a loophole: it's legal to divulge full information about ages, so long as consumers ask for it first.

As the plight of fake news and distrust shows no signs of abating, consumers are likely to become more inquisitive of producers' practices in the long-term and ask yet more questions. Transparency in whisky, though, is about more than just revealing the barley varieties or yeast strains used in a product. Whisky makers that claim to have transparency at the heart of their operation must also be ready to honestly answer questions about company ethics, including difficult, more important topics such as sustainability, their supply chain, HR policies, gender pay gaps, and more.

Consumers value brands and companies that are honest, sincere, and trustworthy. But transparency can't exist in one part of a business and not another. If producers claim that they "have nothing to hide," they must be prepared to prove it.

SEEKING POSSIBILITIES IN SINGLE MALT

by Matt Hofmann

Since I was a child, I've been the type of person that needs to know the "why" behind something. In school I think this made me somewhat of a frustration to my teachers. I needed to understand why something was relevant to me, or why it is considered "true" enough to be taught to me as such. I'm proud to say that I've never outgrown that proclivity. I hope I never do as long as I live.

There's something extremely gratifying about ripping the surface off of something to see what's underneath or taking something apart. Many surrender to that instinct in tangible ways; leave the kid alone in their room long enough and soon their toys are scattered in pieces all over the floor. For me the manifestation is less physical. I want to rip ideas apart. I want to see how they work. What's the structure behind the veneer, even if that veneer is beautiful? Why is it built the way that it is?

What am I hoping to find when I begin to look under the surface? If I'm being honest, it matters less what it is. It's more about the dopamine rush of solving a puzzle, of breaking an idea down into its components then reassembling it. In doing so I gain a greater appreciation for the idea's construction—if logically well-assembled according to my standards, that is. Sometimes what I find is disillusionment to the extent that I'm prepared to outright disregard the components altogether. It's not a toy worth keeping around anymore, the poor construction utterly ruining my impression of it. Most of the time though, I fall somewhere in between:

I'll have an appreciation for the idea fundamentally but in the end want to find other ways, big or small, it could be built better, for me.

At Westland, this is how we view single malt whiskey. Certainly nobody is looking at single malt today and suggesting that it's broken per se. By every estimable metric, this industry is in the midst of the most successful period in its history. Distilleries from across the globe can't fill bottles fast enough to meet the demands of consumers clamoring for the darling of today's whiskey world. The old adage, "If it ain't broke, don't fix it," is not terrible advice to follow. Yet, boom times don't curb our impulse to take it all apart and study it with a critical eye. While it might be obvious that something broken calls for the scrutiny, some of us believe that we have an obligation, a duty almost, to do the same for something that's seemingly working perfectly well. Only then can we identify what might be missing and ultimately learn what should, or might possibly, come next.

> *"There's a thrill that comes with the unraveling of something that, on the face of it, seems to be completely figured out or finished."*

There's a thrill that comes with the unraveling of something that, on the face of it, seems to be completely figured out or finished. At this moment we can recognize the ideal place to begin our journey into the philosophical wilderness. It sits at the magical intersection of the why and the how. The sense of opportunity and possibility, the feeling that we are now exploring Our West, this is what Westland is all about. I've often heard eau-de-vie distillers who produce an unaged spirit made from fruit say that their job is not unlike that of a photographer. Their objective is to capture an aromatic "image" of a fruit at its perfect peak of ripeness. The whiskeys that we release at Westland are something akin to that—snapshots of our journey through time and ideological exploration, sometimes right at the edge of the unknown. But we are not portraitists, we are adventure photographers.

For a few of our whiskeys, these moments we capture are outposts on that boundary, points marked on the trail to show ourselves and the world how far we've come and where we might want to go next. In particular, the Outpost Range collection of whiskeys is meant to capture snapshots from our three most exciting paths of exploration: barley varieties and agriculture, local *Quercus garryana* oak, and Pacific Northwest peat. After just a few short years of inquiries, we have already been convinced that single malt could indeed go further than where it is today. At the core of our conviction is a firm belief that the future is in whiskeys that express a true sense of place. Here in the Pacific Northwest, we are blessed with the tools of the natural world to make it possible.

As we carve a trail through the unknown, we work with the natural terrain of the idea, not against it. That might mean the trail bends and weaves, switches back on itself, or finds itself at the occasional impasse. That trail may not be the most direct route through the wilderness of the unknown, but for sure it means we get to take in the sights on the journey through it. In doing so, we find the occasional natural landmark, a place where the trail stumbles upon something really beautiful. Something worth slowing down long enough to snap a picture. With each annual release of the three whiskeys in the Outpost Range, we share those pictures with all of you.

> *"It stems from a passionate interest in the idea of single malt whiskey—an obsessive drive to better understand how it works, how it could be made better, and how to make it our own."*

Making whiskey this way is something of a selfish proposition, I have to admit. It stems from a passionate interest in the idea of single malt whiskey—an obsessive drive to better understand how it works, how it could be made better, and how to make it our own. There's a history of making single malt, yes, but not here in the Pacific Northwest. As such, the structure behind the idea, the why of its construction, may be less relevant to us here than it is in Scotland. All the more reason to find a way to make it more germane to our culture and to begin to think about how we may do so.

Most of the whiskey industry is incentivized not to take something apart to see if it can be built better. Many in this business are simply not given the license to take it apart, let alone imagine a new way it could be put back together. Some who have the access and skills to examine the idea in its deepest detail may be completely content with its construction, happily putting it back together the same way it was built when they came upon it. I don't begrudge any of them their approaches.

But not us. Freed from any obligation to act as momentary torchbearers of a cultural construct so as to uphold age-old canon, we can simply run into the woods and explore. We can afford ourselves the time and the space to sit down under our favorite tree and begin to take the idea apart, looking at it from a perspective that we can comfortably call our own. Then we begin our trip into Our West. With the Outpost Range, we're able to bring you the best snapshots we can, capturing an idea of why we think single malt could be made better, and how we are actively trying to do so.

WHISKEY FOR A NEW WORLD | 186

THE BIRTH OF A CATEGORY

by Matt Hofmann

Some people think we're nuts. While the idea of Americans producing single malt whiskey is not necessarily crazy in and of itself, the fact that we've bet our livelihoods on it, on a future that most never even considered; this many think a fool's errand.

Others suggest we're ahead of our time. Or at least of the time. They see a group of distilleries forging new ground with brashness, skill, and resolve when the others questioned our very sanity. They celebrate our ambitions as we plunge straight into the unknown, guideposts and safety nets left far behind. Certainly this might not be the conventional way to enter the generations-old whiskey business. But we are not conventional. We are Americans.

Perhaps portraying the whole thing as so audacious is a bit dramatic. But ultimately that's who we are, us Americans. Self-assured and confident with an unwavering bravado. It is undeniably a key part of our cultural DNA. Sure, being so headstrong can put us in choppy waters from time to time. Without it though, we wouldn't even be here.

This culture of audacity has been a hallmark of the American story. How did those who came before us arrive here? What drove them to leave behind all that they had known, those literal and figurative guideposts, and venture forth into an unknowable future? What did they see out here that so many could only just imagine? In truth, we will never know if our forebears fully grasped the weight of their contribution to what would become the great American journey. But as long as we continue to push ourselves forward, on our own personal journeys, we will honor and build on this ethos we have inherited.

So why do we make single malt whiskey—one of the most old-world of traditions? The easy answer, though only partially correct, is to say that we do it because we must do it. We are compelled to pursue it because to do so is in our bones. But there is more to it than that, as of course there always is. As Americans we have always been naturally inclined to challenge conventional thinking. Again today we find ourselves in another state of cultural transition. We don't take for granted what has come before—even traditions we have now invented ourselves—and we do not blindly assume what came before is right. We continue to question everything. As a society we are becoming ever more thoughtful about all things that cross our path and today we expect more from ourselves and from the products we invite into our lives.

The American Single Malt movement is a manifestation of these ideals. America is adding its own voice to the history of whiskey. And while we honor many of the traditions of the old world, we aren't replicating the formula. Instead, we are questioning the way in which we should go about it. For Westland, these fundamental questions were posed in the very early days. "Why make Bourbon if the Northwest is one of the best places in the world to grow barley?" "Why should we limit ourselves by employing the same type of malted barley used in every single malt distillery in the world when others exist?" "Why simply mimic a wood program that was built on economies and traditions of a long-past era in a region thousands of miles away?" For us, the answers to these questions led us to making single malt in the way that we do. For others in this country, the questions (and almost certainly the answers) may be different. This will lead them down a different path and towards a different truth. "If I live in the Southwest and we traditionally smoke with mesquite, why should I use peat?"

It's one thing to ask the questions, but it's another to answer them with action. The courage to act—even when doing so contradicts convention—

is a central characteristic of American ambition. This is the leap we're taking into the unknown. This is what will inevitably make a mark on the world of single malt. Is the reason that we are answering these questions with action, with our products, due solely to American confidence? Or are we intentionally, callously thumbing our noses at tradition and history for the sake of our own egotism? Fundamentally, I don't believe we are acting disrespectfully. But I'll admit, perhaps we're less precious about tradition than other cultures. Where would tradition get you on the frontiers of the new world? When it came to life-or-death decisions which, for many, marks part of their American origin story, would you stick with traditions if it meant you might lower your odds of survival? Innovate or die. Perhaps this was the decision facing our ancestors. It's pretty clear what choice they made.

> *"If being in this melting pot means we've left the rest behind, it might be easy to think that we've got nothing to bind us together. But of course we do have something..."*

If I'm being honest, I'm actually a bit jealous of the traditions of the old world. In tradition you find meaning, you can find an identity. Even now as I write this I'm midway through a series of books exploring the Celtic culture of my Irish ancestors. I think we all struggle with finding an identity—both personally and as a society. One of the difficult things that we experience here in the United States, especially out West, is coming to terms with the idea that we really don't have a long heritage or tie to the old world. If being in this melting pot means we've left the rest behind, it might be easy to think that we've got nothing to bind us together. But of course we do have something—something that makes us Americans, not just in name. We have a shared motivation to take the leap into the unknown.

This, then, is our identity. An oversimplification of American culture this certainly is but there is truth to be found here. If our identity or our culture is to be manifested in our whiskeys, then how does it express itself? Excitingly, the answer is not in simply replicating the whiskeys of the old world and sticking "American" in front of it on the label. Instead, we must interpret the specific physical attributes and consider how a new equation is balanced. The weighted value attributed to each of the forces of traditional whiskey-making, combined with a leap into the unknown and how many questions are asked and answered along the way, this is where it all comes together. This is what we distillers across the country are doing under the banner of American Single Malt.

The end result is less a style of whiskey and more an assemblage of new perspectives on a centuries-old tradition, informed by unique values and influences. Each distillery producing single malt in America is balancing the equation a bit differently. While this may seem like many different "styles of one" have emerged, the reality is that we are all linked together by our willingness to set ourselves down a new path. The identity is in the path; the destinations, the whiskeys themselves, can simultaneously be different and valid.

It's hard to grapple with the meaning of it all while we're busy simply staying on a ride that's just begun. The birth of a category—a rare thing in its own right in the world of spirits—sometimes derives from happenstance, and often times comes with an acute lack of self-awareness. How lucky we are. The category is unfolding with a thundering beauty that I cannot help but absorb with awe. The meeting point of ideas developed through centuries of practice and tradition from the old world with a culture destined to carve its own path. Somewhere within this maelstrom of clashing cultures and ideas is the future of American Single Malt. However, that undeniable desire to stare into the chaos and see where we are headed, this is what marks American Single Malt as American. Not in the future, now. This is American Single Malt Whiskey.

We believe American Single Malt is the next big thing in whiskey. The American Single Malt Whiskey Commission was formed in response to the growing need for American-based producers to define the category—both domestically and internationally—in order to protect, educate, promote, and ultimately grow it.

FOUNDED: March 2016

FOUNDING MEMBERS:

- Balcones Distilling
- F.E.W. Spirits
- Santa Fe Spirits
- Virginia Distillery Co.
- Westward Distillery
- Copperworks Distilling
- Headframe Spirits
- Triple Eight Distillery
- Westland Distillery

CURRENT MEMBERSHIP: 176 distilleries

MISSION: Establish, promote, and protect the category of American Single Malt Whiskey

STANDARD OF IDENTITY:

- Made From 100% Malted Barley
- Distilled Entirely At One Distillery
- Mashed, Distilled, And Matured In The United States of America
- Matured In Oak Casks Of A Capacity Not Exceeding 700 Liters
- Distilled To No More Than 160 (US) Proof (80% Alcohol By Volume)
- Bottled At 80 (US) Proof Or More (40% Alcohol By Volume)

THE PACE OF PROGRESS

by Dave Broom

As humans, we crave the idea of permanence, that feeling that things are fixed. It gives us a sense of reassurance. Our approach to whisky is broadly coloured by the same notion.

While we may accept that the earliest examples were significantly different to what we drink today, it is often believed that since the start of the "modern" Scotch whisky industry (which means 1823), or Bourbon, post-Prohibition, that things have remained the same. Ardbeg has always been what we enjoy now, the same with Wild Turkey.

Of course, that isn't the case. Take Scotch, for example. In the past 100 years, we have seen barley varieties change, the ending of the use of brewers' yeast, lauter tuns and stainless steel washbacks being installed, the virtual ending of direct fire, a widespread switch from worm tubs to shell and tube condensers, a shift from predominantly ex-Sherry casks, to ex-Bourbon. Every single one of those has impacted flavour.

Drinkers' palates have changed as well. The blends which made Scotch a worldwide spirit in the early 1900s (themselves lightened to suit Highball drinking) are nothing like the blends available today. Scotch has been responsive to technology, a drive for efficiency (that started in the 19th century), and consumer demands. It isn't fixed, it is mutable. It would be wrong, therefore, to think of 21st century whisky as being an example of a weary old category finally starting to move forward. It has always done that.

What has happened, however, is that the rate of change has accelerated. In those ancient times (actually the 1990s) when "whisky" meant Scotch,

Bourbon, Irish, and Canadian, it may have seemed that progress was slow, if non-existent. Now every country where distilling is legal is making whisky. From being the speciality of a few territories, it is, for the first time in its 600-plus years existence, a truly global spirit. The newcomers, the young generation, have given the category a new, rapid momentum.

It would be convenient to point to one event which triggered the start of this new world of whisky, but life isn't as neatly packaged as that. Rather than one big bang, there were a series of smaller explosions around the world which helped to shift mindset and build momentum. One of those was the arrival of Japanese single malt on to the export market. The country had long been an enthusiastic consumer of its own whisky. So much so, that there was no need to sell it abroad (this also necessitated the importation of bulk whisky from around the world—but that's for another discussion). All of that changed after home sales collapsed in the late 1990s. With a stock surplus to deal with, Japanese distillers began to sell their single malts in Europe. What was revealed was a subtly different approach to whisky-making. Identifiably single malt, yet different. Flavours were precise, intense, and yet discreet. The methods of production were similar to those employed in Scotland, but again with subtle tweaks. In 2001, Whisky Magazine summoned the great and the good of the industry to a double blind (flights and whiskies not revealed) tasting of its top-scoring whiskies from the previous two years. The overall winner was Yoichi 10-year-old. That day, though unnoticed at the time, the whisky world changed.

"Rather than one big bang, there were a series of smaller explosions around the world which helped to shift mindset and build momentum."

In the US, the genesis of a new approach could be traced back to pioneers such as Old Potrero in 1993, and California's St. George which started its whisky project three years later. It is little coincidence that both were run by former brewers—Fritz Maytag and Lance Winters. From the 1980s onwards, there had been a shift in thinking about beer in America, a reaction against the industrial beer brands. Whisky being made with a craft brewer's mentality— different yeasts, kilning temperatures—shifted the paradigm. The change had also come from within Scotch. The collapse of the blended category in the 1980s had seen the mass closure of nearly 60 distilleries.

Part of the reaction on the part of the majors was to help build the already existing, but tiny, single malt sector. The wider availability of a greater number of single malts introduced a new generation to a drink which was different to the one their fathers and grandfathers drank (and, yes, whisky was very much seen as a solely male drink in these days).

It is funny to see how many origin stories of new distilleries share similar themes.

SCENE 1: *Daytime.* A group of friends are on a weekend away (fishing, skiing, hiking).

SCENE 2: *Midnight.* Sitting around a fire (a regular trope), drinking a bottle (or more) of single malt Scotch.

SCENE 3: *3am.* "I've got an idea. We could make our own whisky."

SCENE 4: *Two months later, a phone rings.* "Remember that distillery idea? Let's do it."

It lies behind the starting of Lark (Tasmania, 1992), Mackmyra (Sweden, 1999), and Stauning (Denmark, 2006), the last of which started in an old butchery using repurposed equipment—a cold store, meat smoker, mincing machine, and brining tank. In Europe, existing distillers, making fruit spirits or genever, also began to include whisky in their offering. All brought their own sensibilities to the project creating a new web of flavours. Single malt Scotch may have been a trigger for many of them, but they were not copying it. Existential questions were asked: What is our whisky? How do we define it? How do we define ourselves? The answer, from all, *"Not Scotch."*

What could we take, what would we change? What could our whisky taste like, what should it taste like? Questions, questions. If the whiskies were to succeed, it was a given that they had to be of high quality. They also had to stand out in a world already filled with distilleries that had a 100-plus year head start. If the principles of production were more or less the same—cereal, yeast, distillation, ageing in wood—what made the whisky different, what were the tangible differences?

One of the answers to that was, "It is from here." For a spirit which had for decades played up heritage and founders' names, it was strangely rootless. This also fitted in with a wider sense of post-millennial dissatisfaction with a commoditised and homogenised world, and the glimmerings of a new food culture where flavour and local mattered. Could spirits be part of that?

Look around your town. What's missing? Who are the local producers, where is the market, the flour mill, the brewery…the distillery? Was this nostalgia, or an attempt to build something new? Probably a bit of both, but it has led to deeper questions being asked. If Bourbon can be made anywhere in the US, then what would Californian or Minnesotan versions be like? Would they reflect their place of origin?

Around the world, distillers are responding in different ways to that question. "This whisky comes from us and our approach," they say. "But it's also made in these conditions, with these ingredients which are local." Not terroir, but more akin to a bioregional approach.

A bioregion, Alan Thiem Durning explains, is "a geographical unit more real in an ecological sense than any of the lines governments draw…" It is defined by watersheds, climate, flora and fauna, but also the way in which these factors have influenced the human culture of the area. It's not new. The Scottish planner and ecologist Patrick Geddes outlined the idea in the 19th century.

"If you know what is taught by plants and water, you are in on the gossip and can truly feel more at home," writes the poet Gary Snyder. "…To know you are [at home] is to realise that you are part of a part, and that the whole is made of parts each of which is whole. **You start with the part you are whole in.**" [Author's emphasis.]

Conditions impact what grows around you and whether you grow barley, rye, wheat, or corn. Then, what variety of each are you using and what flavours might they have. What of using heritage varieties—Bere barley in Scotland (Bruichladdich) or Jimmy Red corn in South Carolina (High Wire).

If there is peat around you, then what are its properties? The peat in Tasmania and the Pacific Northwest are different from each other in composition—and therefore aromatically—just as that of Islay is not the same as that on the Scottish mainland, Ireland, or Denmark. If you want to use smoke and there is no peat, then what smoke is used in your food culture? Scrub oak (Texas), chestnut (France, Germany), manuka (New Zealand), mesquite (Arizona), nettles (Denmark), sheep dung (Iceland)? What trees grow around you? Is the oak species different? Is the flavour different when it's made into a cask? Does the cask have to be oak? How do the conditions affect maturation?

Flavour, distillation, and a cultural approach can then combine in different ways. Look at the different flavours of rye whiskies coming from The Netherlands (Millstone), Germany (Stork), Austria (Haider), Finland (Kyro), New York State (Empire Rye), Pennsylvania (Wigle), Canada (Lot 40), and more recently, Scotland (Arbikie). All rye, but the angle of approach could be based on a culinary background (mainland Europe), other spirits (genever), a reinterpretation of distilling heritage (US and Canada)—or widening the remit of 'whisky' (Scotland). The flavour differences are as wide as you might imagine.

"Thinking such as this is underpinning the approaches taken by today's most forward-thinking whisky distillers."

Thinking such as this is underpinning the approaches taken by today's most forward-thinking whisky distillers. Even as many resist the idea that there should be legislation defining a regional style, the nature of place still pervades the way in which they talk whisky. As one distiller said, "I don't want to make whisky in Texas, I want to make Texan whisky." The result, thankfully, is diversity rather than parochialism. "To become intimate with your home region, to know the territory as well as you can…does not prevent you from recognising the diversity of other places, cultures, ways," writes another bioregionalist thinker David Landis. "…Local knowledge is the grounding for global knowledge."

Forward movement can often be thought to mean that the old ways are being left behind, but it is not a binary choice. Rather, as one Japanese papermaker said to me, "Today's tradition is yesterday's innovation, today's innovation is tomorrow's tradition."

So take ideas from beer (kilning, yeast types), look at Scotch but also Japan, adapt and work with different distillation techniques, look at raw materials (oak, grains), work with crop scientists to produce new strains that give flavour and yield. Some distillers take some of these; Westland, uniquely, applies them all.

Whisky-making is a continuum, and in the new whisky world, the past is as important a generator of ideas as a genuinely new approach. So, today, there are new Irish distillers consulting 19th century mashbill recipes (Boann, Dingle, Blackwater), English distillers finding a repository of old cereal varieties entombed in thatched cottages (Oxford Artisan), while Todd Leopold has reinvented the American tradition of the three-chambered still. The realisation that different strains of cereal can be flavour drivers has also re-established a chain between farmer, maltster, and distiller which had been broken. With it has come the appreciation that whisky is not an industrial product, but an agricultural (or more accurately, agri-cultural) one.

In all whisky styles, (single malt, Bourbon, rye, single pot still) the template established over years becomes a palimpsest, new writing over the older texts which remain there, embedded. The arrival of the new whiskies has also presented Scotch with a challenge—how to redefine itself within a new whisky world. Can it be cognisant of what is happening, be willing to learn lessons from this new generation, and innovate? Can it reflect place in a way which isn't clichéd? It has, and it can. Occasionally you still hear, "We're the biggest category, and therefore the best." But in single malt, the focus is increasingly on distillery heritage and flavour, rather than the often spurious history and the cold dead hand of marketing.

Scotland's newest distilleries—InchDairnie, Torabhaig, Ardnamurchan, Nc'nean, Raasay—have more in common with their colleagues around

"The arrival of the new whiskies has also presented Scotch with a challenge—how to redefine itself within a new whisky world."

the world than they have with the 200-year old rivals at home. Most are in remote, underpopulated locations and their arrival has helped to revive and rebuild fractured communities. How will this new world of whisky evolve? Will we see an identifiably Australian style, or a Nordic one? What of England, France, Argentina, Iceland, New Zealand? It's too early to say. In some cases, American and Australian single malt for example, legislation will be required.

The consumer will change as well. The days of whisky being a drink only for men have long gone, as many women are whisky drinkers these days. It is also a drink for 20-somethings not just 50-somethings. It is consumed neat, long, in cocktails. Who is drinking it, how they are drinking it, and the influence of wider societal trends will all have an impact. Distillers will have to remain nimble.

Flavour will remain the prime motivation for drinking, but behind that will be sustainability. In terms of production, links to agriculture will deepen, new techniques will be invented or adapted, new flavours explored, and the past will continue to be mined. Location will play an increasingly important role because conditions and a sense of place will always matter when dealing with a spirit that is so reliant on provenance. New stories will be told. Change will continue. It is inevitable.

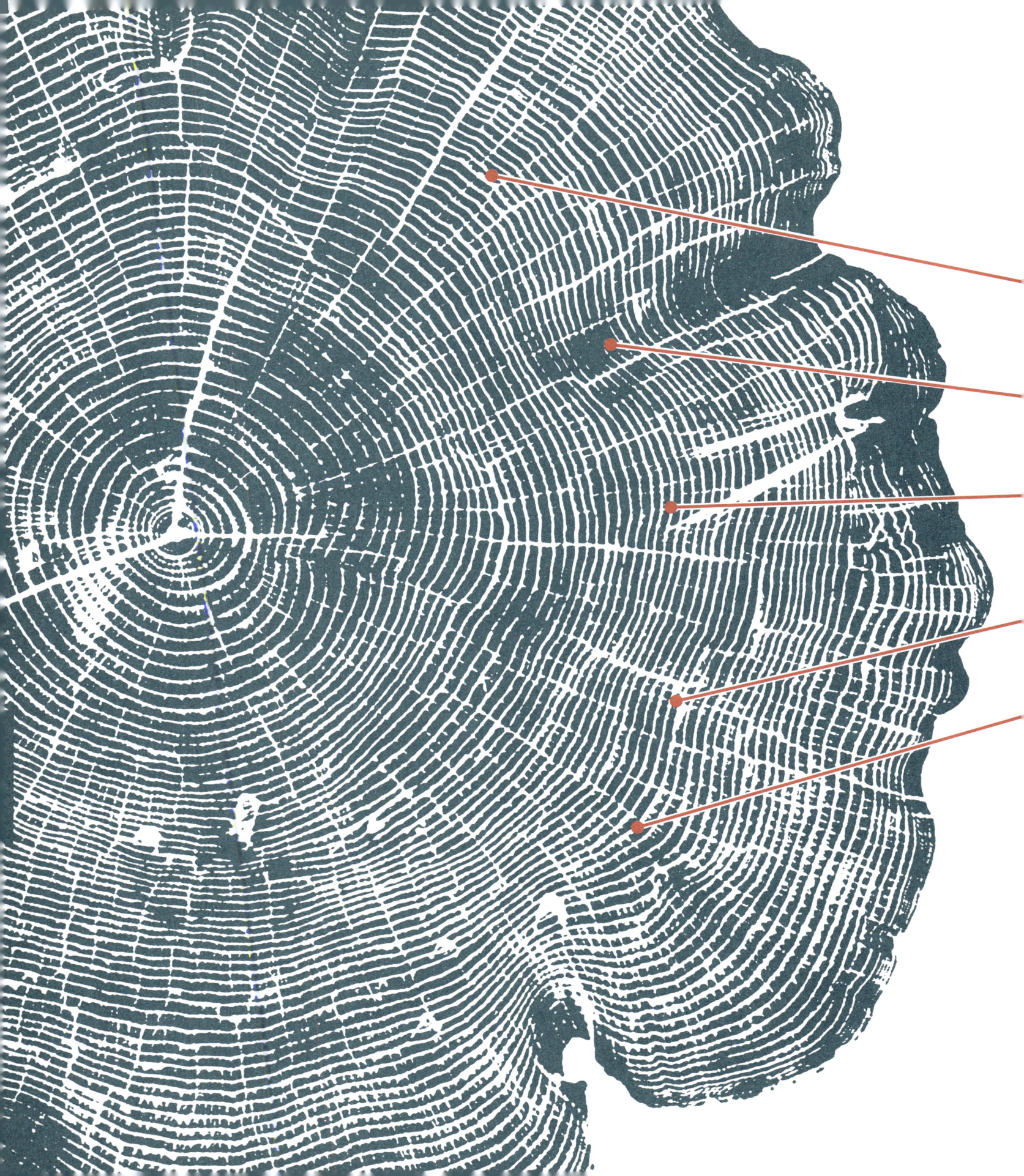

HEADS DOWN AGAIN

THE PROGRESS OF WESTLAND 2018–2019

Every year we have new ideas, too many to pursue with the time we're given each day. We've had to make choices, commit to a relative few if we wanted to meet our standards in the end. By 2018, our sights were squarely set on just a couple transformative concepts that would lead us in our next decade as a distillery. It's in the trenches though, where few can see, that you plant the seeds for the future.

1. MARCH 2018: WHISKY MAGAZINE AMERICAN MASTER DISTILLER OF THE YEAR
While it's a title Matt has always been uncomfortable with, it is the taxonomy of our industry and a burden he must bear. That burden becomes a little lighter when you're named top in the nation.

2. APRIL 2018: ULTIMATE SPIRITS CHALLENGE CHAIRMAN'S TROPHY
Winning once is an honor. Winning again is an honor and a pattern.

3. AUGUST 2018: FIRST CASK EXCHANGE RELEASE
In what has become a beloved (and coveted) series, our Cask Exchange program with local Pacific Northwest breweries brings a whole new dimension to our pursuit of provenance.

4. NOVEMBER 2018: REVERIE RELEASE
This bespoke limited bottling quickly became a cult favorite amongst Westland fans, proving that creativity in blending is no longer a lost art form.

5. OCTOBER 2019: WSU BARLEY FELLOWSHIP GRANT
Westland furthered its investment in barley research by fully funding a PhD student to focus on developing new varieties of barley specifically for whiskey, and while doing so prioritize farmers, flavor, and the environment.

WHISKEY FOR A NEW WORLD | 204

WHISKEY FOR A NEW WORLD | 206

WHISKEY FOR A NEW WORLD | 208

PART SIX

EPILOGUE

"We shall not cease from exploration, and the end of all our exploring will be to arrive where we started and know the place for the first time."

—

T.S. Eliot

A SERMON FROM THE DEACON SEAT

by John B. Larson

The life of a Northwest logger has always been punctuated by the wet. Tin pants pelted with rain, a choker passed through mud, a misery whip slickened with kerosene, a steam-belching donkey thirsty for water, a Mackinaw shirt drenched in summer sweat. These were hallmarks of loggers' long days spent bringing down the towering fir, cedar, spruce, and hemlock that blanketed the region. Loggers worked, spit, ate, drank, slept, and played in a world defined by the wet. They preferred stepping into caulked boots still damp from the day prior—dry leather was too stiff. They craved the moist zing of fresh Copenhagen—three-week-old snoose was unacceptably stale. And they savored a long tug of whiskey whenever the opportunity arose—good whiskey found in a deep-woods logging camp was preciously rare.

In the decades abutting the turn of the 19th century, when Northwest logging camps swelled with Midwest transplants and Scandinavian immigrants, loggers were quite literally on the cutting edge of a region's transformation from untouched rainforest to working timberland. As the late renowned author Murray Morgan titled it, this "last wilderness" was a vast, timbered land butted up against the Pacific Ocean, teeming with young men eager to make their mark on the landscape. Armed with the ubiquitous crosscut saw and sporting calf-hugging cork boots, these men were hired to accomplish the seemingly impossible task of toppling and moving giants.

Though the jobs were physically intense, finding woods work was as easy as showing up with a strong back and the proper attire. Demand for labor in the logging camps was as constant as the tidal flow of water into and out of the region's log-choked waterways. A typical camp consisted of 30 to 40 men with practically poetic job titles: faller, bucker, chaser, choker setter, bull buck, whistle punk, donkey puncher, hooktender, rigging slinger. These were the jobs that took men each day from the relative comforts of camp to the toil and danger of the logging show. When in full swing, this crew could move heaven and earth bringing out the big logs that sawmills so feverishly demanded.

Donning their ubiquitous cork boots, wool shirt, suspenders, tin pants and jacket, loggers maintained a uniform of sorts, one that was eminently functional. The pin-like spikes that protruded from the soles of corks could grip even the slickest moss-covered log. Wool helped stave off the chill even if drenched from a passing downpour or a day-long drizzle. Suspenders and tin pants worked in tandem. In his now classic treatise on Grays Harbor's logging history, *They Tried to Cut It All*, Edwin Van Syckle colorfully painted a picture of such loggers. These "hairy-eared giant-killers with chips in their gizzards and pancakes in their craws" were clad and characterized in the following manner… "Their boots would be spiked, their pants stagged, and their wool underwear would rasp an ordinary mortal raw. They would be the roaringest, cussedest, ring-tailed hell-benders ever to pass from one paradise into another."

Those workers that remained in camp were equally significant to the operation as a whole. The bullcook, the flunky, and the saw filer were essential when it came to keeping a camp intact and moving harmoniously. Without good grub and without sharp saws, you had mutiny. Loggers required—no, demanded—good food and plenty of it. Modern day dieticians have estimated a required daily intake of nearly 8,000 calories by loggers of this early era. Likewise, a faller or bucker wouldn't stand for a dull or poorly sharpened saw—the proper set of cutter teeth and the finely hammered edge of rakers could not be compromised. As such, saw filers were camp nobility, maintaining their own specially-built shacks replete with windows and skylights for optimum light with which to perform this precision work.

Though logging camp life has often been romanticized in the decades since this heyday, one glaring fact cannot be ignored. Logging was deadly. Loggers were killed and wounded at an alarming rate and newspaper accounts of the carnage were almost daily throughout the region. Even though such news in this era of budding national industrialization was commonplace, it remained tragic. In the early 1920s, Washington maintained an average of 17 loggers killed each month—and these only included those that were accurately reported. The injury toll was exponentially higher. Such statistics reveal an industry driven overwhelmingly by production at the expense of worker safety. It is no wonder that loggers needed a stiff drink to wash away the memory of a fallen fellow worker's death or to soothe the aches and pains of this physically grueling profession.

Despite all this, logging camp life still merits some romanticizing. If one had the capacity to simply accept the dangers of the work, there was a unique sense of identity associated with being a logger. These men had to be individually tough yet collectively cooperative. They needed great physical stamina, mental fortitude, mechanical ingenuity, and, of course, indifference to working in the wet. Camp life fostered lasting bonds that bridged ethnicity and language. Camp life forged friendships and built trust amidst the life-threatening work. There was a sense of shared mission amongst loggers that prompted competition within a company's various camps as well as between rival companies. The desire to work hard was infectious.

> "Camp orators claimed the Deacon's Seat as a place to regale fellow loggers with stories of near mishaps in the woods or a recent 'logger's delight.'"

But hard work also requires rest and, naturally, evening time was cherished in the camps. When his day's work was done, satisfied with a dining hall feast as darkness descended, a logger sought comfort. Parking himself on an old crate, a half-hewn log, a rough milled plank—the proverbial "Deacon's Seat"—the Northwest logger here found camp camaraderie. He made and played music, dealt cards, danced, read books or a week-old newspaper, and generally tinkered around his tent or bunk car. Camp orators claimed the Deacon's Seat as a place to regale fellow loggers with stories of near mishaps in the woods or a recent "logger's delight," (an extended wild night on the town). Camp visitors were invited to occupy the Deacon's Seat as a welcoming spot to relieve weary traveling feet. Camp hunters used the Deacon Seat as a stage for exhibiting their trophies. In the decades before Prohibition's attempted erasure of intoxicating liquors from camps, the Deacon's Seat was where a bottle was passed and whiskey flowed. Fundamentally, the Deacon's Seat—central to logging camp life—was a place to recharge.

The Deacon Seat's traditional roots hail from much earlier East Coast camps. In *A History of Lumbering in Maine, 1861-1960,* historian Dave Smith noted that "in front of the bunk was found the Deacon Seat. This bench, made of logs about 15 inches through, split, shaved smooth, and mounted on legs, was the social center of the camp. Here, in the evening, the men would sit, talk, smoke, and discuss the day's work." As East Coast forests were logged off and loggers continued their western migration, the Deacon's Deat moved with them. Historian Joseph DeLaittre recorded the seat's presence in his 1959 *A Story of Early Lumbering in Minnesota*, "The sleeping camp had bunks, one over the other, filled with straw: the Deacon Seat was built along the foot. There was a long stove in the center which was fired with four-foot wood…" In Northwest coastal logging camps, the Deacon's Seat took on a decidedly less formal appearance. Loggers here were not so concerned with tradition and prided themselves on their adaptive use and reuse of what was at hand. Gone were split logs mounted on legs. An old dynamite box would do. Gone was the seat's smooth shaved top when a rough sawn plank or split cedar board would suffice. It's worth remembering that the Northwest logger was a breed all his own—these "ring-tailed hell benders" were masters at making quick and effective use of what resources were readily available.

Symbolically, however, the Deacon's Seat was more than just an object on which to relax. In this turn-of-the-century era of Northwest logging, camps were necessarily transitory. As one unit was logged off, another was being cruised. When a camp picked up and relocated, another Deacon's Seat was fashioned for the crew to settle on anew. In an industry that ruthlessly and randomly used up its workforce, the Deacon's Seat served as a nightly reset button, allowing men to rise day after day to set another choker or buck another big fir. It was said the life expectancy of the Northwest logger was no more than seven years working in the woods. Some lasted mere days. Others survived a lifetime. For those who cheated death and lived to tell their grandchildren about life in the camps, luck and good fortune were decidedly on their side. For this fortunate lot, the Deacon's Seat was there at the end of every work day like a trusted friend. It gave these men the strength to rise again each morning to persist, survive, and thrive.

EPILOGUE | 220

221 | OUR WEST IS WHISKEY

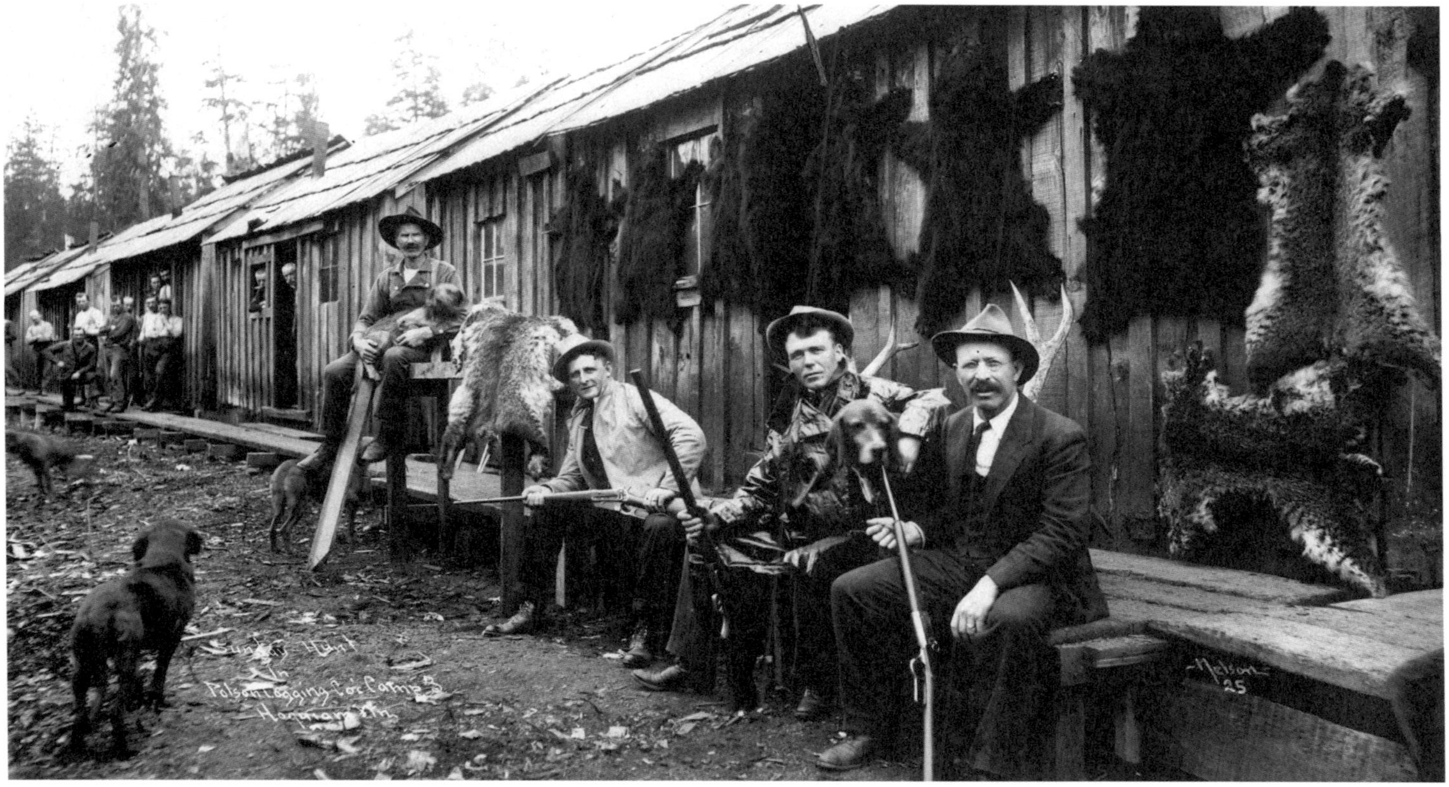
Hunt
In
Polson Logging Co. Camp
Nelson
25

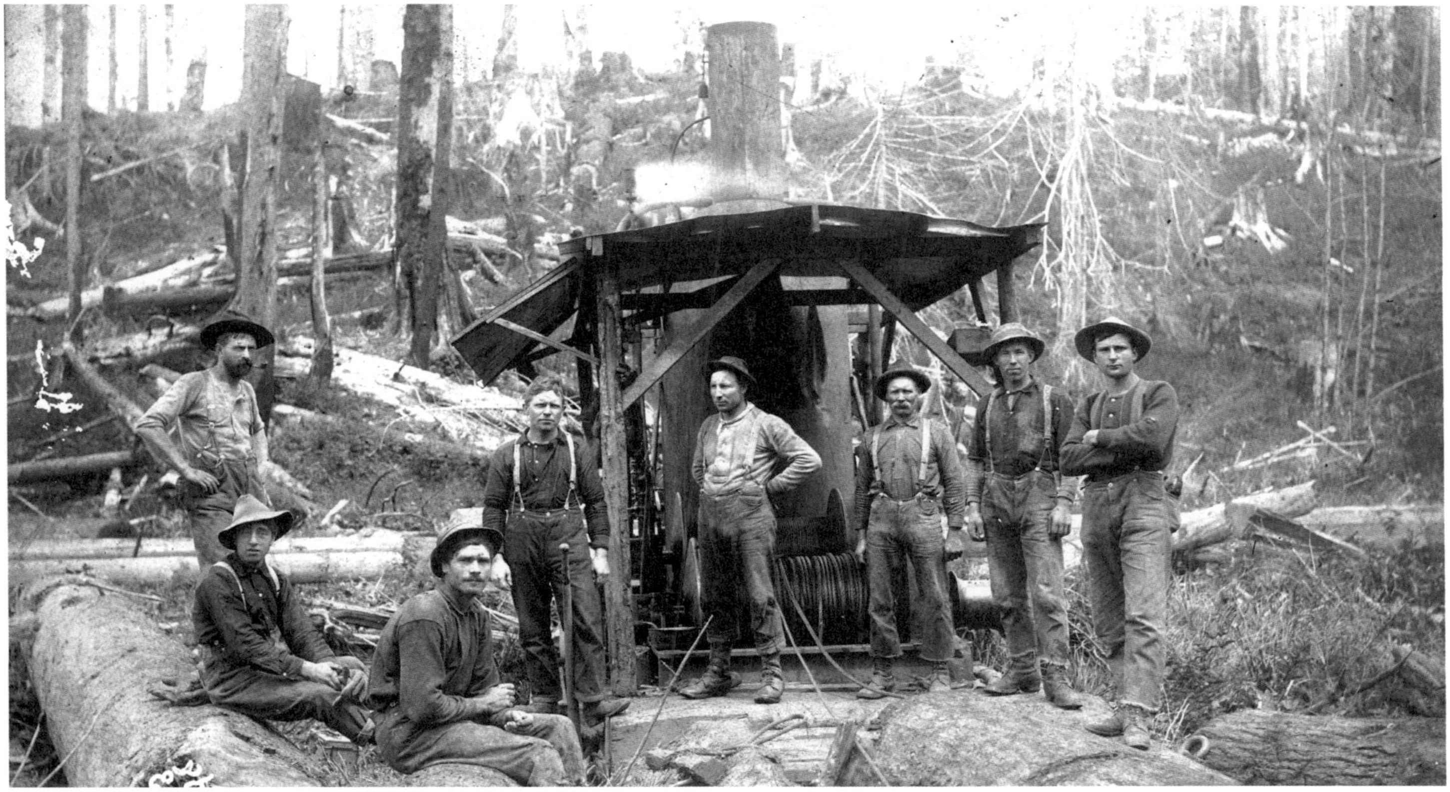

INTO THE UNKNOWN

by Matt Hofmann

The end. That's what you're supposed to find at the back of the book, right? Except this book isn't so much a self-contained story as it is a snapshot of Westland as it stands. It's only a moment in time. We have ten years behind us with hopefully many more to go. Certainly, the work is far from done.

I'm sipping a dram of Colere Edition 1 as I write this, giving me something like barley-colored glasses with which to find a new perspective. The aroma, which I can neatly describe as the whiskey equivalent to a Grand Cru white Burgundy, is something new for Westland and for our fans. We've committed, at least initially, to utilizing only used oak casks for maturing all of the whiskeys we think are destined for the Colere series one day. We believe used cooperage, rather than virgin, will give us the ideal balance between the more subtle flavor notes of unique barley varieties and the notes we get from the cask the whiskey matures in. The idea of balance has always been a part of our "house style," our whiskey DNA, and this first edition of Colere is no exception. It will, however, be a slightly different manifestation of that type of balance. The same philosophy is at its core but extended into new realms of possibility based on what we have in front of us.

Colere's contribution to the larger picture of Westland's house style is a microcosm of what is happening across the entirety of the company. We are driven by the same intrinsic ethos, the same sense of possibility and opportunity that was present at the outset of this endeavor. That will never change, for it is fundamental to Westland as a company. But that ethos is simultaneously what causes the manifestation of Westland to change, to evolve. What you see in product will change over time, if slowly compared to other industries. The change isn't necessarily the point, but it is the consequence of a culture that compels us to continue examining the idea of what single malt is, and what it can be if we dare to imagine it.

Occasionally along a journey it is best to stop to examine, to take stock of where we've come from and where we're going. To celebrate this moment in time we've also created two new whiskeys. Westland American Single Malt will be the new flagship expression for us in most marketplaces worldwide, the entry point into our universe. A second and new iteration of Deacon Seat, each bottle released with one copy of this book, is the other. We released the first edition of Deacon Seat back in 2013. It was meant to signify our vision for where we were headed, made with whiskey that was informed by where we came from. We picked ten of the most exciting casks we could find and made a bespoke whiskey that acted as the starting gun of what we knew, even at the time, would be a very long race.

"Occasionally along a journey it is best to stop to examine, to take stock of where we've come from and where we're going."

This second bottling of Deacon Seat finds us looking back with reflection on a much more immediate interpretation of where we've come from, one that is much more tangible. It's not so much a case of 'what our culture and heritage has inspired us to do' as the first edition was. This is more so informed by the idea that 'this is what we've done with that inspiration to date.' It is also a soothsayer of sorts, portending where we want to go next. I've mentioned earlier in this book that our approach to whiskey-making is akin to that of an adventure photographer, exploring through Our West and cataloguing the progress along the way. Deacon Seat, and this book along with it, are a time capsule—a way for us to collect some of our favorite images, reflections on the past, and notes on our hopes for the future. It will surely be outdated, even by the time this goes to print, but it is an honest effort to capture a moment in time and bring you in closer to see our dreams for the future.

What are those dreams? Where to start…

Genuinely, this is a challenge. When you are on a journey to explore the unknown, you don't simply "find it." You usually just find more of it to explore, the options often times overwhelming you. That's what it's like to be at Westland today. But that means we're still alive, the mission as exciting and as relevant as ever.

By the time this book goes to print, Westland will have also planted its first barley crop on its own farm (or we will have tried and failed!). At the time of this writing, the farm is still something of a secret to our fans out there. It has become the next logical step for us to understand the core subject matter of single malt whiskey—malted barley—and to look at it from a new angle and to pursue its possibilities. Getting our hands dirty at this small scale, approximately ten acres of barley, will help us better understand the plight of our partners in the farming and malting community.

We are also dedicating acreage from this farm to support the research of PhD student Louis Prager, who we are funding through a fellowship program in conjunction with the Washington State University Bread Lab. His research, focusing on finding barley varieties that are economically viable for farmers in the Pacific Northwest, grown with sustainable farming methods, and chosen for flavor novelty rather than conformity, will benefit the universe of barley across the United States, and likely beyond.

"We act as expectant mother, midwife, and screaming newborn all in one."

At a larger scale we are also working to steward the emerging category of American Single Malt Whiskey. Our goal collectively is to establish the foundation of this new category and promote it. In this crusade, Westland stands out front to lead. Participating in the creation of a new category is something of a surreal experience, even in an industry as slow-moving as single malt. We act as expectant mother, midwife, and screaming newborn all in one, simultaneously giving birth to a new style of whiskey that includes us, yet also goes far beyond just Westland. I almost don't dare to imagine what it could ultimately grow up to be, but we must. A bottle of American Single Malt Whiskey on every serious backbar in the world would make us both happy parents and giddy children. And that would only be a milestone, albeit a great one, along the way to a type of category maturity that could fundamentally alter the idea of what whiskey means at a global level.

If you're sensing a pattern here, you're catching on. Words like "growth," "opportunity," and "build," are there for a reason, yet they are not forced either. We saw the potential in single malt whiskey ten years ago. This faith has only been strengthened by what we have learned to date and what we see from where we stand today. Like our ancestors before us, we saw the West ahead of us at our founding and were encouraged to explore. Only now we're deep into the wild of it, invigorated not by what we've passed through but what we see ahead of us, as well as what we sense lies just out of sight. We can't wait to find out what the next ten years have in store for us, and for what we can share with you.

EPILOGUE | 228

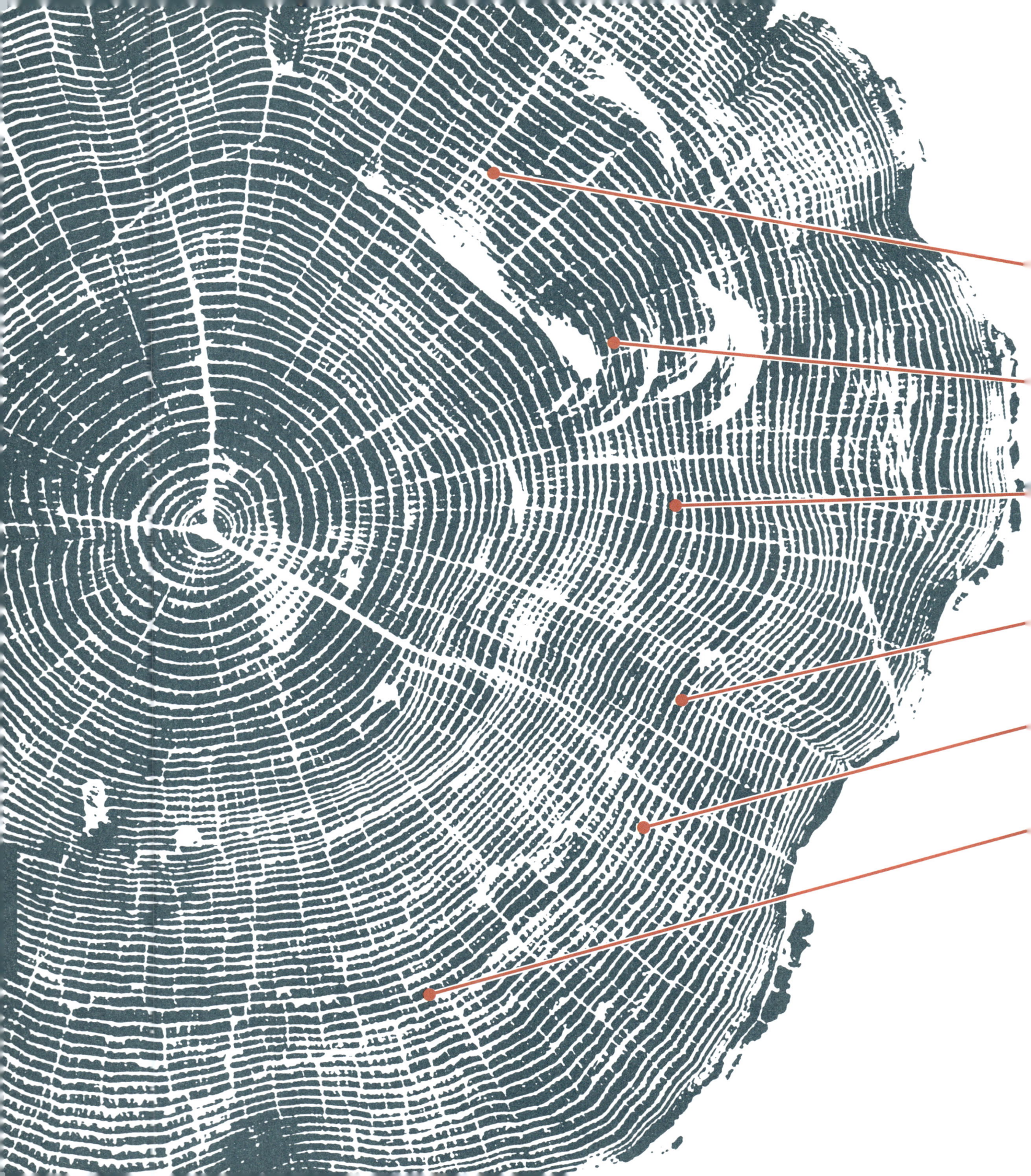

TEN YEARS

After a decade we look backwards and forwards, reveling in the moment ever so briefly. We are humbled by the reception we've received from the world of whiskey and thrilled to have surrounded ourselves with such a passionate community of single malt lovers. But our work is far from finished. In fact, it seems like we're still just getting started.

1 FEBRUARY 2020: WORLD WHISKY FORUM
We had the great honor of hosting the World Whisky Forum in Seattle. Bringing together the most revered and innovative minds in whiskey, Westland was at the center of the dawning of the next great age in whiskey.

2 FEBRUARY 2020: COLDFOOT RELEASE
With this limited bottling we brought together two iconic Seattle brands in Westland and C.C. Filson to tell the story of exploring possibilities at the edge of the known world.

3 MARCH 2020: WHISKY MAGAZINE DISTILLERY MANAGER OF THE YEAR
In a role typically hidden to most, our very own Scott Sell was recognized for his monumental achievements in building America's first great single malt whiskey distillery.

4 MARCH 2020: SKAGIT VALLEY FARM PURCHASE
Further committing to the valley that has given us so much in return, Westland purchased an 80-acre property to house our new rackhouses and grow barley for both research and production.

5 JUNE 2020: OUTPOST RANGE LAUNCH
The introduction of our Outpost Range of single malt whiskeys which includes limited annual bottlings of Garryana, Colere, and Solum, is arguably the most important milestone of any in Westland history; one that has been years in the making.

6 MARCH 2021: SKAGIT RACKHOUSES COMPLETE
Skagit Valley will now be the home to all of our whiskey stocks for generations to come.

2020–2021 THE PROGRESS OF WESTLAND

EPILOGUE | 232

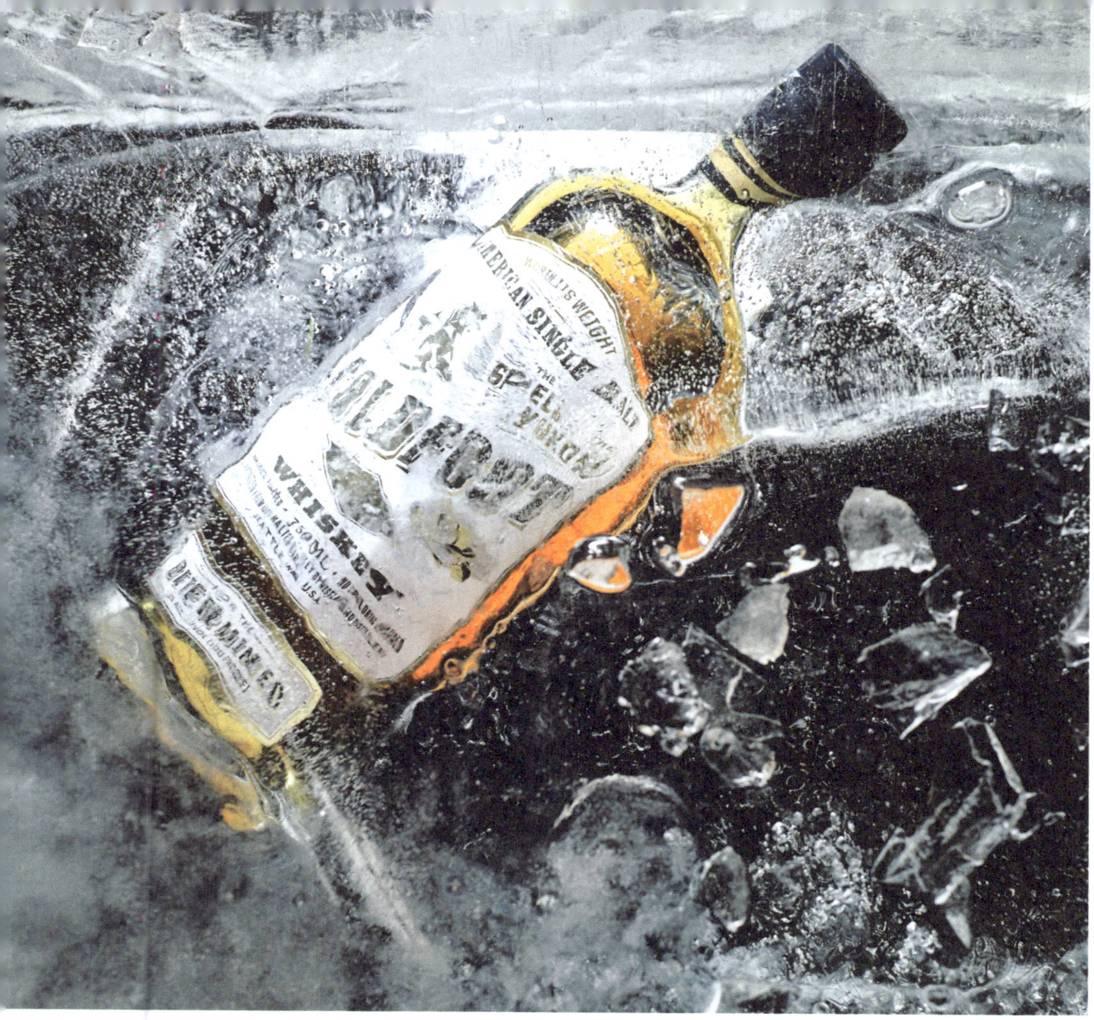

"Go forth to the highest north, till a lonely trail ye find..."

LISTEN TO THE WILD

FOLLOW THE LONELY TRA

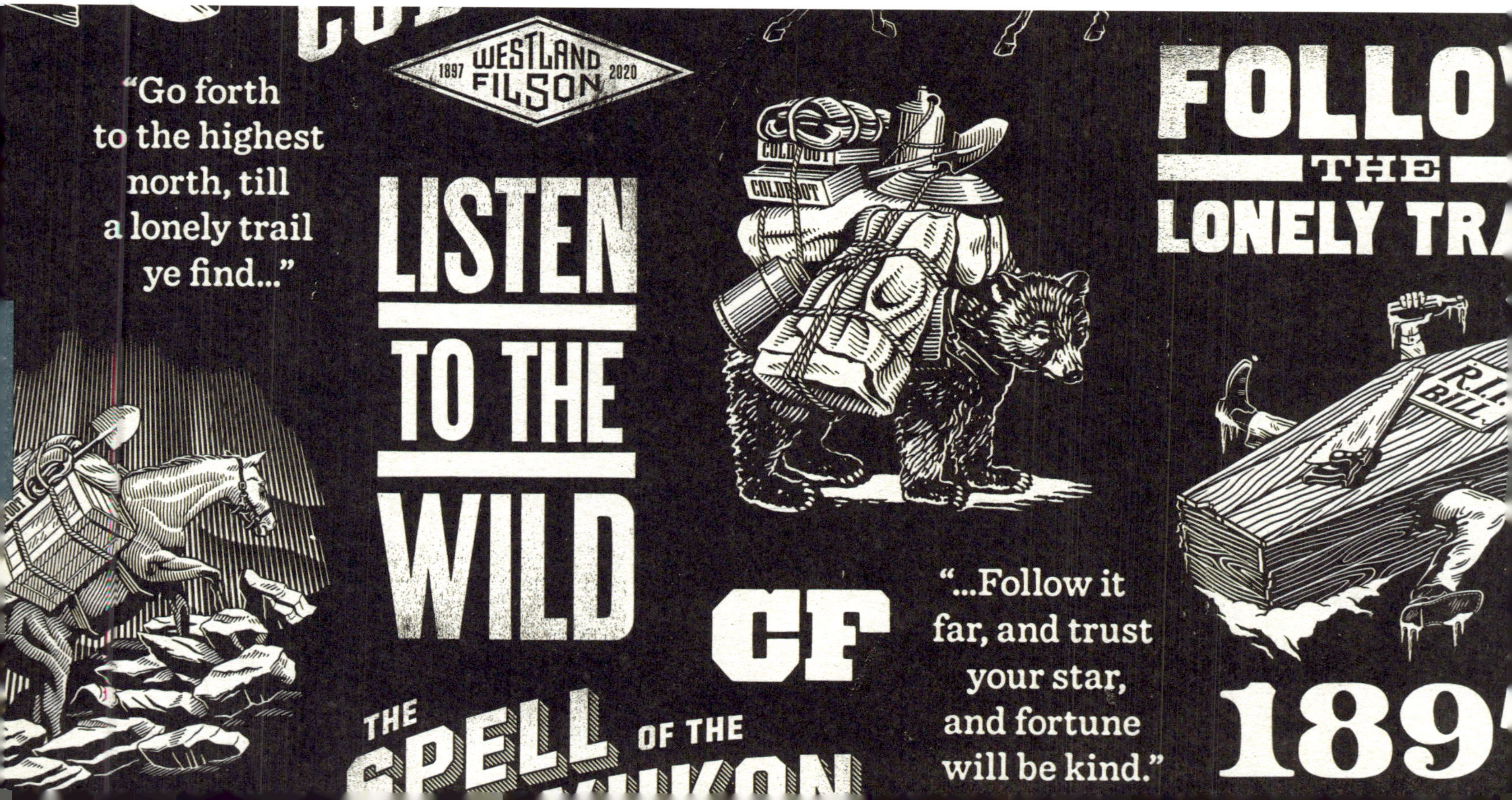

CF

"...Follow it far, and trust your star, and fortune will be kind."

THE **SPELL** OF THE **YUKON**

189

EPILOGUE | 234

EPILOGUE

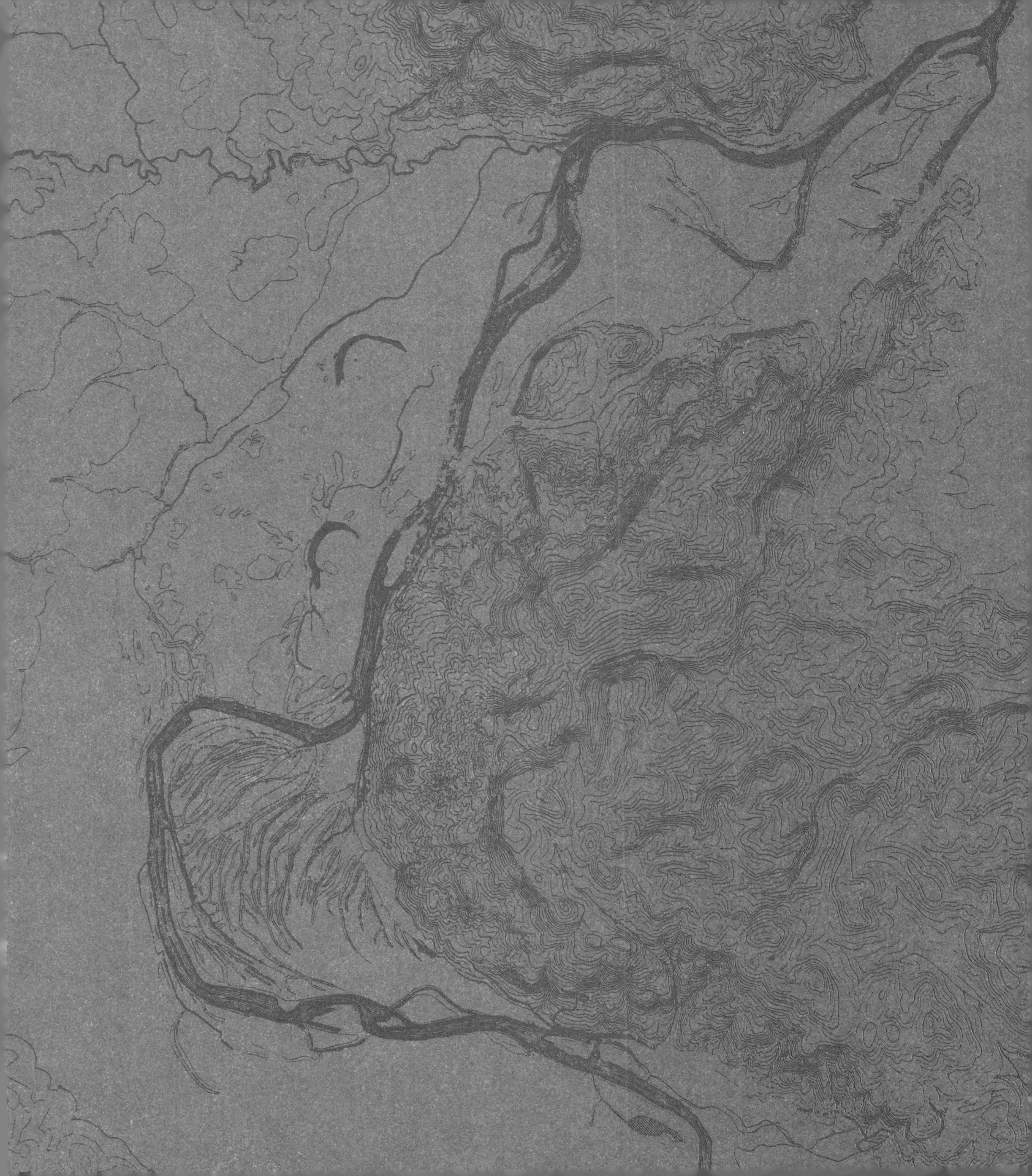

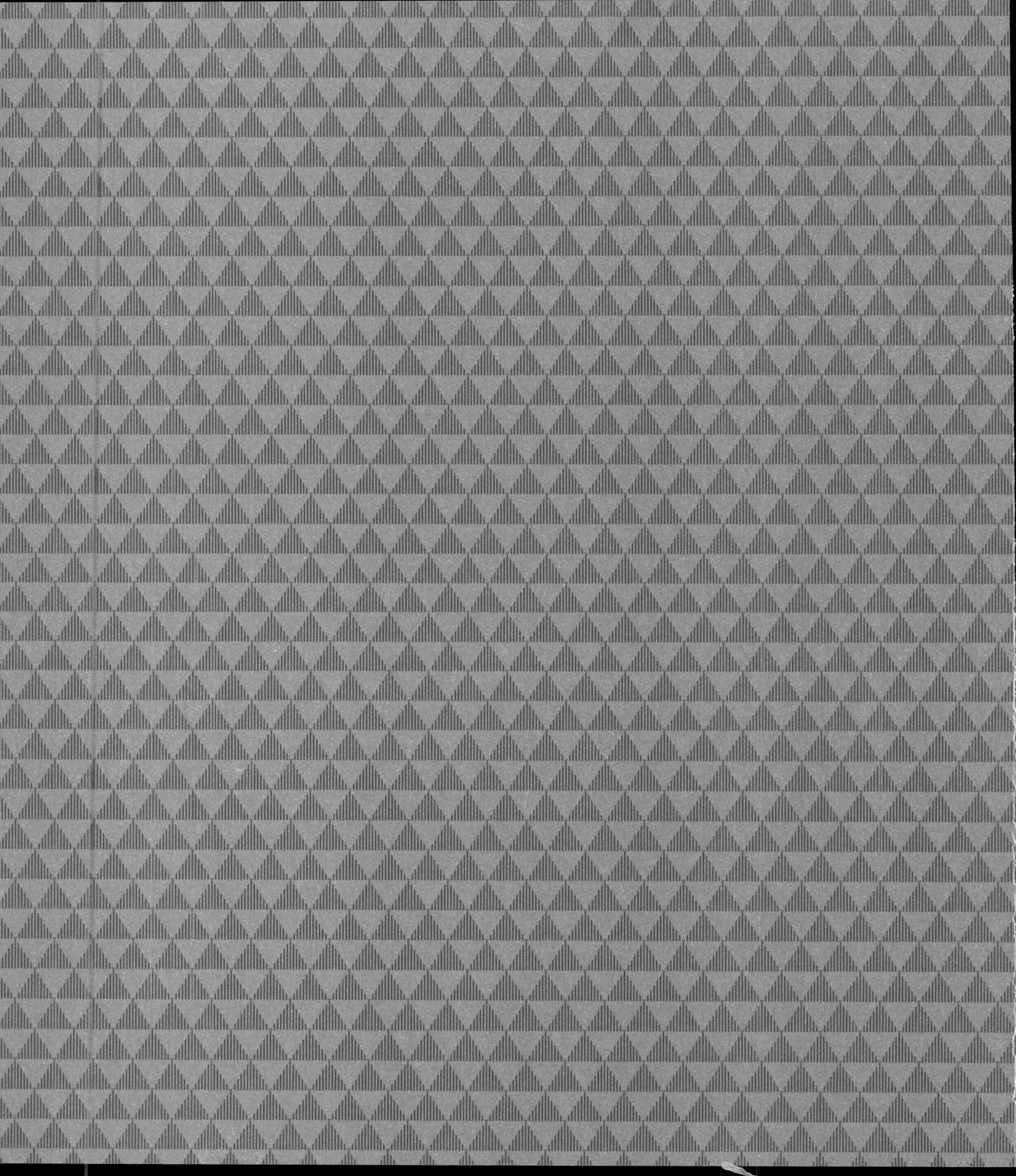